Dan Burkhardt

LIFE WITH FIORELLO

THE MACMILLAN COMPANY
NEW YORK · CHICAGO
DALLAS · ATLANTA · SAN FRANCISCO
LONDON · MANILA

**THE MACMILLAN COMPANY
OF CANADA, LIMITED**
TORONTO

FIORELLO H. LA GUARDIA

****

LIFE WITH
FIORELLO

A Memoir by
ERNEST CUNEO

****

The Macmillan Company

NEW YORK · 1955

The New York Press Photographers Association photographs are selections from an album compiled by the Association commemorating the Mayoralty years of Fiorello H. La Guardia and presented to him shortly before his death. They were taken from the files of the *New York Times, New York Herald Tribune, Daily News, Daily Mirror, PM, New York Sun, New York World-Telegram, New York Post,* Acme Newspictures, Associated Press, and International News Photos.

"Life with Fiorello" so well portrays him that I read it with deep emotion. The scars of battling for and with Fiorello set forth in this book by Ernest Cuneo were part of their close association and friendship. It was a period of changing times, and Fiorello, giving his all to his work, needed the kind of companionship and devotion that existed between them.

Whether in Congress or as Mayor of New York City, Fiorello devoted himself to making life happier and easier for the greater number, not always a popular thing to do, so there were many heartaches and disappointments, but his wonderful sense of humor, so well described in this book, helped to lighten the task.

I am so happy this book was written, because Ernest Cuneo portrays Fiorello as few knew him.

Marie M. La Guardia

FOREWORD

In the fall of 1951, four years after the death of Fiorello
H. La Guardia, I received a call from one of his old Congressional office staff, of which I had been a member, invit-
ing me to a memorial luncheon. It was to be something of
an occasion. Various awards were to be made to those who
had most advanced the cause of good government, especially in municipalities, and various distinguished speakers
had been asked from all over the country. The La Guardia
Awards in this cause were, I thought, well named, for no
man in American history had done more to erase what
Lord Bryce called America's worst stain, municipal corruption.

But I was glad to go for other reasons. Twenty years had
passed, and a good deal of water had rolled over the dam,
as well as a cascade of blood over the world, since we of his
old Congressional force had last assembled. I had last
seen Fiorello himself in Paris in 1946. He was a world-
famous figure then, and had been for many years. His activities as Mayor of New York were constantly being re-
corded in headlines, films, and legend; City Hall hadn't

confined him. During the war he had occupied all sorts of national posts, starting with Director of the U.S. Office of Civilian Defense and going on to include a dozen other assignments, some of them top secret. When I saw him in 1946 he was head of UNRRA, working like a Trojan at the job of feeding a war-exhausted world.

When I entered the huge room on the second floor of the Astor Hotel, I found it packed with the sort of audience he used to address. So pervasive was his personality that I half expected to see him presiding. The turnout was in itself a tremendous tribute to Fiorello, considering the beautiful fall weather outside. There were a lot of people I knew and a lot I didn't. Some I knew by sight. By and large, they were earnest, public-spirited people of deep conviction. For one reason or another Fiorello had been for all of them a champion and a rallying point. To that degree, at least, there was about the gathering the atmosphere of a Saxon earl's funeral, a massing of banners, a conclave of chieftains at the noble Chief's bier.

There was some awkwardness at first while people sought their component groups. This was not surprising. Fiorello was a many-sided man: his letters and records, for example, are more voluminous than those of all the other mayors of New York combined. He expressed himself fully on all the major issues of his time; as a result, whole segments of his supporters had no notion of other segments in other areas, though in the true Brahman sense, he was to all of them the same man. There wasn't much mystery about Fiorello.

The speakers, who were also the award recipients, were from many large cities, excellent people all, but they were

what Fiorello never was—deadly dull. The affair slowly
turned into an interminable State Occasion, a sort of sol-
emn declaration at a national shrine. Fiorello would have
hated it. I could see him rolling his eyes to the ceiling and
stroking his chin ruefully, a mannerism conveying that he
was in a purgatory of boredom. And boredom, to Fiorello
—the least boring of men—was more painful than to lesser
mortals. Those of us who had worked closely with him
knew that life for Fiorello was an endlessly exhilarating
affair, full of the sound and fury of combat. But even his
love of battle was only part of his sheer joy in life itself.
Fiorello lived hard every minute, reveled in every second.
The over-all atmosphere he created was one of tremendous
vitality, of bursting, healthy gusto punctuated by expressions of monumental disgust, gargantuan laughter, scathing
denunciations, or unbelievably extravagant praise. His word
pictures were painted in the boldest of primary colors;
there were no pastels, no in-betweens. For example, if he
liked my brief—that is, if it supported his view—I became
the Crown Prince of the Realm, a future President of the
United States; if he didn't like the brief—that is, if it disagreed with his view—or, worse still, if it raised bothersome
questions, he would manifest his anger by exhibiting a
mock-solicitous pity for me, asking if I felt all right, offering
to get me a glass of water. This would invariably be followed by a short, violent attack on the educational system
in general, lawyers in personam, and "precedent" in particular. Precedent: how he hated the word! If the objections
I raised were feeble, he might not speak to me for several
hours; if they were both cogent and valid, sometimes he
wouldn't talk to me for days.

My experience was by no means unique. All of us in that Congressional office force experienced moments of anger, exasperation, and humiliation at Fiorello's hands. Each of us had known the exaltation of being on the Mont Blanc heights of his praise at one moment, only to be plunged to the Dead Sea depths of his disdain at the next. Each of us had heard himself proclaimed by Fiorello as the flying clipper ship of an advancing civilization, only to be charged the very next day with being a despicable barnacle on the hull of the great ship Progress. But underlying everything else was a solid foundation of profound respect and affection we were not ashamed to call by its right name: love. Our love for him was something like that of the Old Guards' for Napoleon. The aura around him had more the clangor of arms and the camaraderie of a crack assault brigade than of an office force. We were all happy to accept a minimum of security for a maximum of action. Heavy battle could come at any time; our work was often like a cavalry raid into enemy territory. Fiorello not only shot the works, he shot them from the hip. For example, he suddenly told me one late afternoon to draw up impeachment proceedings for Andrew W. Mellon, then Secretary of the Treasury, for use the next day at noon—and, incredibly, Fiorello's subsequent attack resulted in Mellon's being kicked upstairs to the post of Ambassador to Great Britain.

That was the normal tempo of his life—but you would never have guessed it by listening to the memorial speakers that afternoon. On and on they droned, detailing his great civic virtue and his fine accomplishments. They sounded like old-fashioned schoolmarms piously measuring Alexander's armor, as if to find there the clue to the fierce beat of the warrior's heart which carried the armor into battle. As the dull speakers drew the dreary afternoon to its merciful conclusion, I determined to set down my own personal experiences with Fiorello as I remembered them, and only as I remembered them, with all the faults of faulty memory, but with the deepest respect for one of the greatest fighting spirits in American history.

This, then, is simply an informal memoir of the "Major" as I remember him.

His enemies called him a fanatic. There was no doubt that Fiorello was a seized man. At times, he had the fury of a Michelangelo tearing a statue out of the living rock. The rage of creation was often upon him; indeed, it seldom left him. At other times he was an implacable John Brown, fighting for a vision of man's freedom which he alone could see.

The Christian concept of Heaven was very real to him, except that he believed it was achievable on earth and, if he only hurried, possible in his lifetime. He conceived of life as a heroic struggle, with Man against Evil, and himself as Man's champion. Man was always at a shining Zenith in Fiorello's vision. And so, as Man's defender, Fiorello was always fiercely posting westward to hold by main strength the sun up on his lance, that it might eternally light for Man the paths of righteousness, instead of daily and ignominiously compromising with the Powers of Darkness. The intrinsically heroic is sometimes initially ridiculous, but Fiorello's dynamic personality quickly cut through the first stages. People who started out by tagging him a wild-eyed Don Quixote ended by following him as though he were St. George.

Since this is to be so personal a book, it is only fair that the limitations of my vantage point be set forth. When I went to work for him, I was twenty-five, a law student awaiting admission to the Bar, and an ex-reporter for the New York *Daily News,* covering the usual night's grist of the Big City's murders, suicides, fires, and felonies. The Roaring Twenties had just piled up in the Big Crash. My lifeline was my deadline. Newspaper work was in my blood. I loved the express-train speed and the boiler-room noise of the big presses in that slam-bang Billion Dollar Merger, Tiger Girl Shoots Yale Lover era. We were racing the *Daily Mirror* under Phil Payne, and it was something akin to the early Mississippi packet races, with all furnaces roaring and a cabin boy sitting on the safety valves. Yesterday's headlines were ancient history, racing away like the backwash from the ships' paddlewheels.

After the crash we were just young college people, dumped out into a world which had no place for us, and in which we weren't wanted. Too badly hurt to be bitter, we hung on and battled back as best we could; and we got tough awfully early. It was headspinning, the leap from home and campus to the impersonal hard sidewalks, but in the course of the beating we absorbed, we learned an invaluable lesson: they paid off on the score, and you could save all excuses for your Aunt Minnie. . . .

At twenty-five I was an omnivorous reader, fascinated by power and warfare, far more interested in the Field Officers' Manual than in Blackstone. I had taken Clausewitz's Military Tactics and worked out an analogy to the New York Civil Practice Act; I regarded money as a limited part of the logistical system, unfortunately indispensable in manning troops and fleets but a mere accessory in the field of Force. At Columbia I had hugely enjoyed the organ roll of John Erskine's lectures, but it was wise and vivid John Dewey who chartered me free to love the Runyons and the Winchells and the gods of the rolling presses. It was Dewey who provided me with the rationalization for what I would have done anyhow. He legitimized my craving for action, excitement, and competition, giving it the philosophical blessing of Pragmatism. Before long, I realized that the sordid city's tragedies weren't simply Baghdad on the Subway. Not even Life, they were Death. I was willing to believe that the only true life was that of the artist, in medal play against his own talents, instead of match play against his fellows. Which let me out. All my training was in fighting, a dependent art at best, but I was stuck with it. Also, I suffered from good glands, effervescent spirits, and an iron constitution.

My emotional training since I was fourteen had been upon the football fields. This involved the best of equipment, a great deal of personal attention from elders who should have known better, one Herculean effort once a week, vastly and unduly appreciated in the small school community (and never afterward), and the hell with everything else. A sort of pseudo privilege attends all this, pseudo because it only lasts as long as your legs and your right-hand punch, both of which fade miserably in your late twenties, especially if you've got to earn a living at something else.

Fiorello's office reminded me, upon arrival, far more of a locker room at game time than of a mere place of business. If anything, the locker-room combat tempo was stepped up, and I never saw the tempo slacken. If I were telling a Columbia freshman class about him, I would say that Fiorello was the greatest fighting American of our time. Jefferson would have called him brother; Jackson would have embraced him as a comrade in arms; Hull would have wanted him on the *Constitution* and Custer at his last stand. His mark is on every important legislation in the last forty years, and for much of it he fought and broke ground. In the vast cathedral of American history, he deserves stained glass.

This is not, however, a portrait in stained glass, or in library shadows either. Rather, it is simply a candid snapshot of a great statesman and a great friend, taken by a young man blinking in the glare of the City Room and the glitter of New York. I have no desire to apologize for not having written a definitive biography of a subject who so satisfactorily defies definition in any case; my only aim has been to talk in my own way about Fiorello as I remember him, and to suggest as well as I can the magnificent human outlines of the man before they are lost in the well meaning monuments to his great work. Because—in the phraseology of Broadway's supreme accolade—this was one Hell of a Guy.

I

Like some other hundreds of young men who had just passed their Bar examinations, in the spring of 1931 I had to get a job as a law clerk to serve the then required six months' apprenticeship before final admission. This wasn't easy. The depression was in full swing; and even though clerks' salaries were infinitesimal, law firms weren't throwing any kind of money away on beginners. Somehow, though, the Bar requirement had to be met.

In previous summers I had worked as a reporter for the New York *Daily News*, when it was still located at 25 Park Place. I told the other reporters there of my problem, and Lowell Limpus, Night City Editor and a friend of La Guardia's, said he would talk to him about a clerkship for me. Limpus told me La Guardia was terrible but wonderful. He spoke of my prospective job under him with the enthusiasm of a mechanic who had never made a parachute jump assuring a new flier that there was nothing to it. What he said made me feel both hopeful—and distinctly glum.

Not, of course, that Limpus had to tell me much about

La Guardia, whose face and fame were already established in the public mind. I was merely hoping that at close quarters the Iron Man of popular repute might be found to be less formidable.

To the citizens of New York in the Roaring Twenties, Fiorello was as inescapable as the aurora borealis in the life of an Eskimo. He was their Jeremiah. Every time the revelry swelled higher on a new market boom, Fiorello thundered the warning that carloadings were down and unemployment was up—like a riverman shouting to doomed Babylon that the Tigris was rising. He was much more than the handwriting on the wall; he was a neon light on the end of the civic nose. More than a Socratian gadfly, he was an Arizona-bred hornet. He stung the civic consciousness, and the bump hurt.

Monroe's administration was known as the Era of Good Feeling. A hundred years later the Roaring Twenties were an era of seemingly endless High Feeling. It was a golden age of broad prosperity and broader acceptances, an age in which Chicago gangsters maintained a Riding and Saddle Club and New York gangsters shot 70's on the exclusive golf links when they weren't shooting one another. Amid the general rejoicing Fiorello was nothing so passive as a skeleton at the feast. Instead he dragged the skeleton into the banquet hall and thundered an accusation of murder. Above the clatter of the market ticker he was shouting hoarsely: "Is this prosperity—that the self-proclaimed wealthiest nation takes less care of its mothers and babies than little New Zealand?" Or: "Is this rock foundation—when the miners are dying of silicosis?" No social injustice escaped his fierce eye, and St. Jerome, beating the anvil of Vulcan, couldn't have set up a more terrible din.

I knew all this, of course. But in my scheme of things, Conservatives and Liberals were necessary to each other. Further, I had no alternatives from which to choose in 1931. The Conservatives, whom Fiorello despised, seemed to me to be valuable people performing a necessary service—that of conserving the form of things. I liked form, though not enough to spend my life preserving it. The Conservatives, I felt, provided the viscosity and the Liberals the expansion, and their abrasive action on each other resulted in orderly evolution. It added up quite simply. But in any event, the Conservatives weren't interested in a nobody from a small town like me. They were looking for correct young men with connections.

And criminal law was out. I wouldn't touch gangsters with a pole of any given length. Perhaps everyone has to have an outlet for his sadistic contempt, and gangsters were mine. I hated them by background, training, instinct, and observation as a bunch of miserable, cowardly curs.

This left the Liberals, for whom Fiorello was the Plumed Knight. Working with him represented to me a chance for a sword and a shield, a chance in the coming Big Fight. As it turned out, it wasn't a Big Fight at all. The badly frightened Conservatives retreated, put their heads in the sand and their tails in the air. With a heavy assist from Fiorello, F.D.R. subsequently gave them a swift kick which heaved them into the hangover of the Throbbing Thirties. However, none of these abstract considerations were any more immediately relevant to me than the office of the Chief of Naval Operations is to an oil-soaked sailor on a pitching life raft. The nation was singing—or rather croaking "Brother, Can You Spare a Dime," and I had to have a job. More specifically, I had to have a clerkship, however little it paid. Under the circumstances, Lowell Limpus's offer sounded good to me.

Lowell went to see La Guardia and returned in the high state of elation and stimulation that people usually took away after a session with Fiorello. Laughing heartily as he told me about it, Lowell said he had told Fiorello that a young friend of his had just graduated from law school and that Fiorello had said gravely that that was bad, very bad indeed. Lowell had then mentioned the clerkship, and Fiorello had affected an incredulous air, as though he were being asked to contribute to the delinquency of a minor. Limpus had then remarked that my physical appearance at the moment ought not to be held against me. This was before the day when an eyepatch was the mark of a man of distinction; and, as it happened, I was wearing one because of a jagged rip over my right eye which I had got in a post-season professional football game. Fiorello, according to Lowell, was suddenly all sunshine. "Tell him to come see me," he said enthusiastically. "Tell him to come in. Maybe we can save him yet from becoming a lawyer."

My first meeting with Fiorello La Guardia took place at his office at 295 Madison Avenue. I walked down a big marble ramp to the elevators and got off at the sixteenth floor. His office consisted of only two rooms. The outer room contained four typing desks and a long, hard visitors' bench on which several people could sit most uncomfortably. A young man and two young women were very busy at the typewriters. I confided diffidently to one of them that I had an appointment. Someone came out of the inner sanctum in a few minutes, and I was told to go in.

The inner room was medium-sized, with a large desk and three plain chairs. You faced Fiorello as you came in. Facing him, on the wall, was a painting of some very poor children playing ball on an unattractive vacant lot, the focus of the picture being a ragged urchin with his hat turned sideways, at bat.

I stood there in an uneasy attitude of semi-attention while he went on reading something on his desk. Suddenly, without looking up, he jabbed his finger at a chair to the left of his desk. I sat down. Minutes went by. I suffered. What I did not realize at the time was that he intended me to suffer. A clock nearby ticked remorselessly on and on, like a time bomb. I became more and more painfully aware of the ignominy of my position—a mere worm of a law clerk looking for a job. Then Fiorello suddenly looked up with an absolutely flat expression. "What do you want?" he said, tonelessly.

"Lowell Limpus—" I began.

"Yes, I know," he said impatiently. Looking me directly in my good eye, he almost sneered. "Why do you want to become a lawyer?"

"Because," I said stoutly, "I believe in justice."

His square body lunged forward and his black eyes flashed contemptuously. "Who do you think you're kidding?" he rasped harshly.

I blushed and sweated.

He crowded me, like a boxer pursuing the advantage of a very heavy blow. "To live off the people?" he shouted. "To take their earnings? When a decent world comes," he yelled, "there won't *be* any lawyers!" His hunched, menacing figure and the unexpectedness of the attack sparked a reflex action on my part: while I didn't actually move, I found myself measuring him for a left hook if he did come in, and I remember tucking my chin into my shoulder slightly. The whole thing had the eerie quality of a nightmare.

At the very peak of this tension, and with the swift change of pace I later came to know so well, he suddenly broke out into a peal of free laughter. He threw his head back and roared with pleasure. Then he said: "Why the hell do you want to work for me? I'm no lawyer, and I never want to be one. There's no future here." (Actually, the Major was one of the most ingenious lawyers I ever met.)

"I only want to serve a clerkship," I said.

Now he became serious. "You don't know what you're getting yourself into," he said. Then, abruptly, "Ask the boy outside!"

"I'm sure—" I started to say.

"No!" said Fiorello, pointing to the door. "Go out there right now and ask the boy outside what it's like to work for me."

I got up hesitantly. "Go on," he said, putting on his glasses, and returning to his reading, "Go on outside and ask Mimi what it is to work for me. Then come back and we'll talk."

I slipped into the outer room and closed the door silently behind me. To the right of the door sat the young man— Mimi, if I had heard correctly. "Sir," I said, and he looked up. There was a certain wan Chaplinesque look about him that made you want to laugh. He had a long nose and a wide mouth, and he wasn't very tall. The combination of eyes and hair was truly remarkable, the eyes huge and dark, practically velvety, suggesting great suffering, coupled with a kind of triumphant resignation, like a peasant living on the slopes of Vesuvius, doggedly enjoying life in spite of the wrath of the volcano which could and probably would descend on him at any second. Over his rather high forehead his lank, thick hair fell like a pony's mane. In fact, he reminded me of a sorrowful pony as he looked up from his work with the air of a man who maintains his personal dignity through a superhuman expenditure of patience. I was terribly uncomfortable, but there was nothing to do but carry out the assignment.

I cleared my throat. "Sir," I said again, "Mr. La Guardia told me to ask you what it's like to work for him."

He regarded me thoughtfully and said, with great deliberation, "I have worked for Major La Guardia for ten years, and all I have got out of it is a terrible inferiority complex." He delivered this statement in a tone of weary finality.

"Sir," I said miserably, "Mr. La Guardia told me to tell him what you said. I forgot to tell you that. I'm terribly sorry. Of course, you were joking."

"I wasn't," he said. "You can tell him." He looked back at his papers tiredly. "Tell him," he repeated, and went back to work.

I had a terrible feeling of being caught up in a minor Greek tragedy, an unwilling herald shuttling back and forth with dire tidings. Helplessly, I looked at Mimi for support, but he was done with me. I opened the door and went back into La Guardia's office and took the witness chair again. The wait was much shorter this time, only a matter of seconds. Fiorello leaned back and shoved his glasses up on his forehead, a characteristic gesture. "What did he say?" he asked with real interest.

"He said, sir," I said, with a dreadful sinking sensation, "that he had been with you for ten years and that all he had got out of it was a terrible inferiority complex." I felt sick with guilt. In another time I mightn't have felt so awful, but this was the Depression and jobs were tough to get. What if this man were to be fired because of me?

A terrific explosion like an ammunition dump going up rocked me back in my chair. The Major was literally contorted with laughter; he had to rest his head on his hand. At last he stopped and leaned toward me with the glistening eyes of a man who had heard something too good to be true. "Did he *really* say that?" he asked eagerly.

I nodded, completely bewildered. "That's what he said."

Like a swallow darting from the eaves of a barn, Fiorello was out from behind his desk and at the door. He wrenched it open. "Mimi! Did you *really* tell this boy that ten years with me had given you a terrible inferiority complex?"

"Yes," I heard Mimi say, coolly and levelly. Then he plicked the typewriter carriage, and I remember the small slam and the little bell; it seemed to add just the right emphasis.

If La Guardia was incredulous before, he now marveled. "By *God*," he said, "I never knew you had that much brains." Fiorello's tone conveyed that a Star was Born. I peered around the door. Mimi said nothing, but a half-smile twisted the corner of his mouth. He looked for all the world like a half pleased, half proud old pony who had just had an unexpected flower pinned on his mane.

Like the action in *Alice in Wonderland*, the scene shifted swiftly. Fiorello whipped back behind his desk and I was again facing him. His laughter had subsided. "By *God*," he said reverently, "I didn't think he had it in him. You never know." I nodded cheerfully, utterly lost but weak with relief.

Then he swung his glasses, the ear pieces hooked inside his lower lip, and gave himself up to profound thought.

"All right," he said brusquely, "you can serve your clerkship here. But I warn you, there's no future to it." I waited for some details, but there were none. He turned back to his papers. I got up and thanked him, but he didn't answer. I opened the door and stepped out into the other room, my chin up. I felt good. Mimi hadn't been fired, and I had the job.

I looked around and the girls were smiling. Mimi was smiling too. It was the beginning of a long and wonderful friendship with all of them. Later I was to understand their joy and share it. It was the unadulterated joy of relief: Zeus Fiorello was benign that day, and a halo to the messenger that made him so, because there were many days when the black cloud was on the mountain and terrible forked lightning was hurled down, paralyzing souls into rigidity in the very act of striking them down. But all was golden sunshine in the valley just now. As I went to the door, Mimi said, "You're to come in at 9:30 tomorrow."

I walked down the corridor toward the elevator, pondering the obvious. Mimi and La Guardia had had no private words; it therefore followed that I had had the job when I walked in, or Mimi couldn't have told me to come in the next morning. Hm-m-m. But that, I was to learn, was Fiorello. He always knew what he was doing and he always knew where it would end. And he was never more sure of a result than when he was acting in an apparently reckless, even irresponsible, manner. He allowed little margin for error in his calculated risks: he nearly always knew the inevitable end of a fight before he decided that battle should be joined. In dozens of later situations, I would protest to him that he was gambling madly on an uncertain outcome, only to find at the showdown that he had had aces back to back from the very beginning.

I went out onto the street and strode happily up Madison Avenue. I felt good. Buoyant, keyed-up, and eager. The way I always felt lining up for the kickoff.

II

The next morning I was in, of course, on time. So were the others. Definitely, the gay atmosphere of the previous afternoon was gone. I thought at first that it might have been my own slightly over-neat and self-conscious presence, but that wasn't it. Not that the place was gloomy, exactly. It was just that we were all merely gray chameleons, hanging helplessly by our tails until our color was set for the day by Fiorello's mood. He came charging in presently, his black hat jammed down on his head and his chin deep in his collar, the picture of intensity. He strode through our hushed greetings and mumbled something in return into his collar. He walked straight on into his office, seeing but not noticing us, like a driver intent on the road, only vaguely aware of the telephone poles slipping by. He closed the door. I sat at the empty desk, with nothing to do, and began to feel awkward again. The others were working. Tension started to mount; my hard collar, the only one in the office, scratched me.

Suddenly, La Guardia's door was opened violently. We all looked up. He simply pointed to me and closed the door again. It was like a split-second shot in a newsreel. I went in and he motioned me to the chair.

"There were Cuneos down in the Village," he said, and it was plain he expected me to take it from there.

"Yes," I said. "My Uncle Lawrence."

"I remember him," said Fiorello. "He voted against me when I ran from down there."

"Oh," I said, wincing at this lese majesty on the part of a relative. "Was there any reason?" It was a stupid remark, and I realized it the moment I had said it.

Fiorello looked as if he were bitterly considering it. Finally he said: "No, there was no reason. I was a God-damned good candidate."

I murmured something to the effect that I was sure he was, but I don't think he heard.

"He's rich, isn't he?" he asked.

"No, not really," I said, "though I believe he has quite a lot of property. I haven't seen much of him." I hoped he would appreciate my oblique disavowal of my uncle's terrible act in voting against him.

"Your father's rich too," he continued accusingly. "What do you want to work for?" He pronounced the word "rich" as if it nauseated him. It conjured up a picture of a cat surfeiting itself on cream, sweet, slick, and disgusting. Actually, my family had no such resources as he implied. The notion that I didn't have to work was fantastic, but it remained a fixed idea with Fiorello as long as I was with him. "Your family's from Genoa," he observed flatly, "which produces businessmen and bankers."

As there was absolutely no doubt of his views on businessmen and bankers, I took up the gauntlet, as I was intended to do. "And mariners," I said firmly. "Let's not forget the mariners."

Fiorello could tell he was getting under my skin. "A great city," he said with absolutely no conviction.

"Well," I said, "a famous one, anyhow."

"I'll say so," said Fiorello with hearty emphasis. "Famous for breeding the stingiest people in the world." This is an old saw in Italy, carried to the extreme of saying that Columbus had to discover a new world because the bankers of Genoa hounded him out of the old one. I was gritting my teeth with rage, and he was laughing. Then, abruptly: "Here. We have work to do." The byplay was over.

He had a Congressional bill before him. Quickly, he explained to me that he had got the government to build some ships to give work during the Depression. "Now," he said, "the minute the shipbuilding companies got the contracts signed, they lowered wages." He looked at me with the eye of a faithful family retainer who had been callously sold down the river, a man monumentally double-crossed. Then he recovered. "That is, They *think* They did," he added harshly, "but I'm going to make the government break those contracts. Go get me some legal reasons."

I had made up my mind, or more exactly, I had reconciled myself to the fact that working for Fiorello would involve nothing like a mellow exchange of ideas, comparison of hypotheses, or mutual exploration of legal theories. I knew such things would be as out of place here as in the turrets of the battleship *Nevada*. In fact, he gave me my instructions now in military terms. As far as I was concerned he was requisitioning ammunition which he needed in a hurry and which he intended to fire on target. He had given me the coordinates and that was that. "O.K.," he said. "Clear decks for action."

I picked up the papers and walked calmly out, but as soon as I was out of sight I sprinted to the Law Library. I actually felt I was in an enemy engagement, like a stoker in a cruiser. Fiorello could do that to you. In the next two years, I was never out of heavy action, and I gloried in every second of it. It can be argued that passing coal is passing coal the world over, and in no case is it other than a menial job. But sweating naked to the waist, and coaling the boilers of a battlewagon when you can feel the trembling of the shattering broadsides overhead, is something more than mere shoveling. It is a battle, and between heaven and earth there is no thrill quite like it. There was another thing, too, that lifted you: you knew the Captain would fight to the last shell. While there was life in him he would fight, and that is as much as anybody can say of any great battle captain from Hannibal to Halsey.

That morning I had buck fever. My excitement was so great I could hardly settle down to work. When I did, though, the going was rough. I gradually began to feel like a dismounted cavalryman making his painful and tedious way through very rough foothills. The cases simply did not sustain Fiorello, and that was all there was to it. The contracts had been signed, and they spoke for themselves. They could not be broken by the spoken word. True, the *Congressional Record* showed Fiorello's driving force behind the shipbuilding program, and his speeches especially pointed up the benefit of the work to jobless people. But nothing to that effect was in the contracts, and try as I would I saw no help for it but to report as much to Fiorello. I was very disappointed, but not desolated. After all, the Law was the Law. Or so, in my innocence, I thought.

Fiorello held an enviable position at the time. He controlled the balance of power in the Seventy-seventh Congress, and by comparison the man on the flying trapeze might as well have been a frozen figure on a Grecian urn. Fiorello was everywhere at once. He knew power, could handle it and smell it and appraise it from afar. He literally ran the Congress. He ringmastered the Hoover Administration with the ease of Benny Leonard boxing the Senior Class champion of De Witt Clinton High School. He would feint it out of position and slap it back. His bewildering footwork was beyond the comprehension of the Great Engineer in the White House. President Hoover was aghast and outraged by Fiorello's tactics, but Fiorello knew he could hit at will, and he did, often with sledgehammer effect.

I went into Fiorello's office the next morning, sad, but with the assurance of a man standing on firm ground. He looked up. "Well?"

"The contracts can't be broken," I said shortly. "Parol Evidence Rule."

"What d'ya mean?" he purred. I was immediately reminded of a tiger licking his chops, circling closer and closer to the tethered kid—me.

"I mean," I said earnestly, but with much less assurance, "that there is no express provision in the ship contracts providing for *no* lowering of wages."

"It was implied," said Fiorello, "and they understood so, too. Can you imagine *me* going to bat for the shipowners?" He snorted. "They knew the deal."

"The implied condition is not material," I intoned.

"The hell it isn't," he said, cocking a sardonic eyebrow. "You just watch."

"Well," I said, "it wasn't expressed, though it may have been implied. Unless," I continued, a shade sarcastically, "you're going to argue something new in the law: that it was expressly implied."

"That's it!" he almost shrieked. "That's what it was: *expressly implied!*" He was very happy, as if he had been handed the complete solution. I was absolutely dismayed.

"There's no such thing, Major," I objected. "It's a contradiction in terms. It's absolutely ridiculous!"

"It may be ridiculous in the courts"—he smiled grimly— "but watch what I do with it. Get me Rainey and Garner," he ordered, and waved me away. Henry Rainey and John Nance Garner were the Democratic House leaders. The calls were put through to Washington, and I could hear Fiorello rumbling over the phone. I distinctly heard him say, just as if it were a perfectly reasonable phrase, in fact a fundamental of the law, that the wage conditions had been expressly implied. He used the phrase like a battery of French 75's, firing it again and again.

In the days that followed, he whipped his support into line and made it widely known on the Floor and in the papers that he was advancing on the entire shipping industry with mayhem in mind. One morning shortly thereafter, he called me in and pointed to a short article in a morning newspaper. It was a brief story relating how the shipbuilders, after a careful and thorough reconsideration of the problem, had restored the pay cuts. He smiled beatifically and turned to his mail.

What he had done, I discovered later, was to attack, not on the basis of the contracts, but by threatening shipping appropriations generally, with particular emphasis on the mail-carrying subsidy. The shipbuilders were forced to restore the pay cuts under pressure from the whole industry. For me, lesson number one was concluded: Cutting the appropriation is to Government what the rabbit punch is to boxing. It isn't exactly cricket, but it certainly is effective.

This episode marked the first of many occasions that prompted me to speculate on what might happen to Fiorello if he weren't on the side of the angels. But Fiorello always landed on his feet, no matter how desperate his contortions in mid-air. His command of Congress was, of course, a huge asset. But even more important was his own inner conviction that in him the Crisis had found the Man. He was armored with complete self-confidence. Not only was he morally certain he had the right answer; he was equally certain that no other answer was conceivable, except to crooks.

Considering this colossal self-assurance of his, one would have thought that those around him would never have questioned his faith in his own impregnability. On the contrary, we all worried about Fiorello and felt terribly protective about him, idiotic though this may have been. Strictly speaking, I suppose he needed about as much protection as a Sherman tank. Still, for all his aggressive bounce, the fact remains that he engendered in our bosoms a fiercely devoted, almost maternal impulse. Part of it, I think, was because of the nature of the game he played: it was important, it was ruthless, it was for keeps. So very much was so often at stake. And for those who made a fatal misstep and slipped, there was no mercy. So we would watch Fiorello charging like a bull down a tightrope, no nets beneath him, and we would be breathless with vertigo. Perhaps, too, we *needed* to think that somewhere, behind that noisily assured front of his, there lurked a little spot that was vulnerable.

For example, months later Fiorello was served with an order one afternoon to appear the next morning and show cause why he shouldn't be personally enjoined from interfering in a certain labor dispute. I felt very upset, but he just glanced at the title of the action, shrugged, and negligently stuffed the papers in his pocket. I said I thought I ought to look at them, and he brusquely asked what for. To work on a defense for the next morning, I replied. He told me not to worry about it and not even to come down to court, but to carry on as usual in the office. My heart was bursting with pity for him. Practically all of the big downtown law offices were in the case against him. They would come fully prepared, and *he* hadn't even read the complaint. They would make mincemeat of him, humiliate him, I was sure.

I got to the office early the next day, but he wasn't there. He had sent word he was going straight to court. I stood it as long as I could, which wasn't very long, and then rushed down after him. I found him in the courtroom, seated by himself, at the end of one of the back benches. I didn't say anything, just sat down miserably beside him.

"What are *you* doing here?" he said, frowning heavily. "I thought I told you to go to the office."

"I did," I said weakly.

"Well, what do you want?" he grumped.

I just shrugged unhappily. After a while, the case was called, and a dozen lawyers stood up. Flunkeys brought in stacks of papers and books, and there was a scuffle for seats at the counsel table. Fiorello didn't move.

Finally, he whispered to me: "These people don't know it yet, but their big witness, the principal manufacturer, became a fugitive from justice last night. Grand larceny. They haven't got a case."

There was a conference at the Bench. I noted that Fiorello hadn't even bothered to take off his topcoat, and that he carried his hat in his hand, ready to depart. The conference at the Bench suddenly broke up like a football huddle going up to the scrimmage line. As if fleeing a hand grenade, the opposing lawyers dove for their hats and the doors, and the flunkeys scurried away with all the papers and books. It was all over.

Fiorello pretended to be very indignant, on the way back, that I had failed to follow his instructions. He said that of all the people he knew, I was the worst time waster. I felt foolish and callow and very glad.

III

Fiorello always said he refused to descend to respectability, but he never lost an opportunity to ascend to righteousness. This trait might have been exasperating if the principles involved were not always so sound and so uncannily prophetic. An incident concerning Richard Whitney illustrates this beautifully. Fiorello always had the idea that he would like to spend his old age as a teacher in a college, with a Chair of Government or Labor. I think he specifically associated this nebulous plan with the University of Arizona. But apparently the officials of New York University heard of this yen of his and made overtures to him about accepting a professorship in Labor Law. I think the offer was inspired in part by his authorship of the Norris-La Guardia Act, prohibiting preliminary injunctions in labor disputes. Fiorello was interested, but distantly, as a man might be in a Florida vacation while he's neck-deep in work with a New York blizzard raging outside: it was impossible to go, but nice to think about. At about the same time the Board of Trustees of N.Y.U. voted an honorary degree to Richard Whitney, then president of the New York Stock Exchange.

Fiorello sat right down and dashed off a letter to the university trustees, which he showed me. It was brief: "Gentlemen: I note by today's papers that you have conferred an honorary degree on Richard Whitney, President of the New York Stock Exchange. Through what oversight did you overlook gangster Alphonse Capone of Chicago?"

That was all, but it was enough. He said to me, with a mischievous grin, "I guess after this they won't want me down there for love nor money." I agreed. Some years later, I was on the periphery of the tremendous struggle between F.D.R. and the Stock Exchange over the Holding Company Act and the Securities and Exchange Commission. Tremendous efforts were made to reach some sort of a compromise, but it was no go. It was known that a Stock Exchange Committee was coming to Washington to declare war to the finish. They came. At the very moment they were delivering their ultimatum, the ticker stuttered out the doleful news that Richard Whitney, their erstwhile president, had confessed to grand larceny. The committee collapsed—one member physically. And then I remembered Fiorello's letter to the trustees of New York University. At the time of writing it, Fiorello himself had thought it an exaggeration, but it turned out to be nearer the awful truth.

But Fiorello almost always tempered harshness with humanity where individual human beings were concerned —once he had gained his point, that is, and could afford to be magnanimous. For instance, Mayor James J. Walker was under investigatory fire while I was with Fiorello. Foxy, flashy, jaunty Jimmie was a fitting symbol of the dizzy, cheaply sophisticated twenties, and the public had taken an odd sort of pride in him. He was an exotic plant, and the fact that his roots were nourished by a political manure pile of unexampled pungency was generally overlooked. But now he was on a spot, and Fiorello was one of his bitterest attackers. Fiorello charged favoritism in the tax lists, and when he found that some of the most reputable people in town were on the list of reductions he included them in his charges. Scandals involving the Old Age Home and the womens' prisons, graft in the hospitals—all this Fiorello laid at Walker's door, and castigated him mercilessly for it. As a matter of course he went down to City Hall to protest a proposed raise in the Mayor's salary from $25,000 to $40,000 a year. Years later, though, when Walker was down and out and virtually unrecognized by respectable society, Fiorello was instrumental in landing him, not a mere job, but a position in private industry at a salary equal to that of the Mayor.

The most characteristic facet of Fiorello's tender side revealed itself in his strong streak of paternalism. The burdens he assumed and the manner in which he reacted to them gave me the impression that he thought of himself as a kind of universal father. When he spoke of eight-year-old children working in factories, his face, always expressive, took on a look of profound Lincolnesque melancholy, which in turn would give way to an expression of terrible ferocity.

For my own part, I was enveloped by Fiorello's paternalism shortly after I began working for him, and I think he retained a fatherly interest in me long after I had left his offices. Like all good fathers, Fiorello honestly believed in the proposition that "Youth," as he sweepingly put it, was the hope of the world. He would frequently ask me what "Youth" was thinking, in much the same way that people question taxicab drivers in order to get a slant on the ideas of the mythical Man in the Street. I myself held no such glowing views of Youth. I strongly suspected that Youth is glorious only in retrospect, and was grateful that it had to be suffered only once. I quoted Justice Holmes to the effect that Youth was nothing for the simple reason that it was only the possibility of being everything. Fiorello answered this by accusing me of reflecting the discouragement of the times. He said that these Bad Times would pass, and that every cloud had a silver lining. I was once constrained to retort that so had every coffin, and this pleased him mightily, as did most things that contained an element of impudence.

Finding myself a sort of bellwether for Youth, however, I was not above taking technical advantage of the situation. I would complain that if Youth despaired it was because it was shown insufficient appreciation by the Older Generation. Fiorello would look astonished: "Who, *me?*" and I would beat a hasty retreat by answering, "No, my father." Fiorello loved to hear stories about my relationship with my father. The first one I ever told him had to do with my youthful career as a center fielder. My father never came to see me play; he just happened to be passing by, he would carefully explain. If I played badly he would tell me later not to mind, it was only a game. But if I played well he subjected me to a barrage of criticism. One day he saw me bust an important game wide open with a ninth-inning triple. I trotted over to my father's car right away, confident this time of deserved praise. "Your batting stance," he greeted me, "is terrible. You look like a great sack of oats tied in the middle." The old indignation returned as I told Fiorello the story. He chortled unfeelingly. "He was only trying to keep you from getting a swelled head, Ernest," he said. And then, with an owlish expression, he added, "But I'm afraid he failed."

He asked me once how my father acted when I was in trouble. I told him that I had never been in serious trouble but once, and that my father had been wonderful on that occasion. I had just turned sixteen, and was driving one evening a very nifty Hudson speedster which my mother had persuaded my father to buy. A man had been killed recently by a hit-and-run driver in a neighboring town, and there was a police alert on. I was at an actual stop when a man in civilian clothes stepped off the sidewalk and asked me for my license. I asked who he was, and he said he was a marshal. I produced my license. Then he asked for the registration of the car. I produced that. He then ordered me to lift up the hood so that he could check the number. At which point I told him to go to hell, that he was the public servant, not me, and that if he wanted to get his shirt sleeves dirty to go ahead. He did, and as it was dark, it took some time. He burned his fingers on a match and got angrier and angrier. "Satisfied?" I jeered, and laughed. He suddenly slapped me across the mouth with the back of his hand. I got out of the car and knocked him down. There was a big hubbub, and I was taken to the police station. They called my home. My father and my older brother came right down. My father took me off and asked me what had happened. I told him exactly. To my complete astonishment, my father told me I had done the right thing, and to keep quiet. My older brother was talking to a policeman who had once worked for my father, and the cop bustled off. Presently, he came back and said that it could all be fixed up with a simple three-dollar fine. "No, it can't," said my father. When the case was called, he asked for an adjournment until he could procure counsel. The Justice ominously said, "Mr. Cuneo, your boy needs good counsel." "He'll have it," replied my father, and that very night he secured the two most eminent lawyers in the state. The charges were dismissed on motion. "What did your father say after it was all over?" Fiorello wanted to know. I told him my father had said that I was too fresh but that he wouldn't stand for me being fined for something I didn't do. "He was absolutely right," said Fiorello approvingly. "Absolutely. Especially about your being too fresh."

Only once did Fiorello side with me against my father. There was a pretty good semi-pro baseball team in our town and they had some good speedball artists. I used to go down to the park and nag until finally they let me catch their warm-up tosses. Before long I was handling their fastest throws and, since I was only ten at the time, it got talked about. One Sunday afternoon my father pushed his way onto the field, told me to take off my glove, took me by the arm, and marched me away. That nipped a potential John McGraw in the bud, and I was terribly resentful. "He just didn't want you to get hurt," Fiorello pointed out. "One of those speedballs could have killed you." I shrugged. "Maybe so," I said. "But he should have let me take the chance." Fiorello considered a moment and said, very seriously: "I think you're right. I think perhaps he should have."

Fiorello sometimes patronized a modest little upstairs speakeasy after a particularly hard day's work. He was a violent opponent of Prohibition and made no bones about it. Once he made beer on the steps of the nation's Capitol and dramatically demanded that he be arrested. Mr. Hoover disdainfully looked the other way. Like most law-abiding citizens, Fiorello broke the Eighteenth Amendment without ever feeling like a criminal. Indeed, his respect for the laws of the land was so sincere that he believed a single foolish law tended to discredit all the others. Even so, I noticed, when he invited me to accompany him for the first time, that his first words on entering were, "I'll have a license up on that mirror again in a year." And it occurred to me that this grumbled promise was in the nature of a ritual, calculated to ease a slight twinge of conscience.

Before I had a chance to order, Fiorello said, "Ernest, what do you drink when you drink with your father?"

"I don't drink with my father," I told him. "My father doesn't drink."

"That settles it," he said. "Give this boy a ginger ale," he told the bartender, "and give me an Old Fashioned."

Though I very seldom drank—my training habits were still strongly upon me—I took this very badly indeed. I said with some heat that I *often* had a drink, and an Old Fashioned at that, and if it was all the same to him I'd have one right now.

He looked at me quizzically, and apparently saw something in my rebellious face that decided him. He gave the bartender the slightest nod of acquiescence. The drinks arrived, we drank in silence, and I felt pretty good about things. Then he turned to me and said sternly, "Now, I'm going to have another one and you're *not*."

We walked up Madison Avenue together afterward, separating at Forty-fourth Street.

"Good night," I said.

"Good night, Ernest," said Fiorello. "And behave yourself," he added, "or I'll tell your father."

We laughed and parted. He was to use those exact words again and again, sometimes jokingly, sometimes angrily. They were, in fact, to be the last he ever spoke to me.

Aside from the threat to tell my father, there were other catch phrases that would indicate, like barometric readings, how I stood with Fiorello at any given moment. When he was exasperated he would say, "What are they *teaching* in the colleges these days?" And when he was particularly pleased, he would say, "Ernest, you are going to be this country's first Latin President."

But for me the highest tribute, far and away more pleasurable than the first Latin President tag, came when he called me into his office one afternoon to meet an especially important visitor and, waving his hand casually in my direction, said, "This is my son."

IV

The innocuous apple is still regarded with revulsion by thousands of people who will forever associate it with poverty, humiliation, and despair. The stock-market crash of 1929 was a national disaster, and for many years thereafter the country was like a badly injured, half drowned swimmer being dashed again and again by the impersonal breakers against bleak, jagged rocks.

Owen D. Young, Colonel Joseph Hartfield, and others held feverish midnight conferences to save the Bank of the United States, but they failed, and so did the bank. A secret run started on New York savings banks, and 10 billions of deposits melted away like butter on a hot skillet. The run was halted when Adolf A. Berle centralized the banks' credit in a revolving fund, but panic was abroad in the land. In the Midwest the farmers went down like a stone in a pond; a bushel of wheat could be bought with a pack of cigarettes.

The official attitude was one of anxious optimism, but fewer and fewer people found themselves able to share it. The big national magazines ran articles extolling American ingenuity and resilience, citing cases that described enterprising men and women turning adversity into triumph by starting home industries. In actual fact, only a pitifully small percentage of the hardest hit were able to twist the tail of the wolf at the door, pioneer spirit or no pioneer spirit. Yet the medicated Pollyanna syrup was ladled to the public by the bucketful—only the country was too sick to do more than sip it, pluck at the counterpane, and turn its face to the wall.

The misery was intensified by the sharp, ironic contrast to the freewheeling years that had preceded the crash. The twenties . . . What a Luna Park of a world it was then! Most middle-aged people look back on those giddy days with nostalgia—a sheepish nostalgia, perhaps, but none the less real for all that. We remember it with overt or covert affection because the country was young then, young and wild, like a crazy kid, and we were young in it. Viewed from today's chilly vantage point, the twenties seem to us to have been tinged with a curious kind of innocence. We are mature now, "responsible" and "experienced"; but as we keep a watchful eye on the horizon for signs of the first great mushroom in the sky we find it consoling to reflect that once we knew what it was to be gay.

The roller coaster of the twenties was powered by the huge, unprecedented purchasing power of the "masses" —and by the installment plan. The automobile, the radio, the telephone, and the airplane all came to full bloom in a decade, and all of them mightily influenced the mores and folkways of the nation. In place of the candy-striped silk shirt, a snappy motorcar was now the symbol of the good rich life, and its possession became a compelling necessity. People didn't think they had struck it rich; they simply felt they had come into their own. They had that elusive bluebird caged at last.

Some of the symptoms of the times were, of course, extreme even then. One Hollywood tycoon had his press agent ballyhoo his bathroom, which was replete with gold plate and jeweled faucets. When it came to the length of their yachts, industrial magnates were fiercely competitive. The Mayor of New York preened himself in a smart mink-lined overcoat. A special body was built for the car of a tall Cabinet officer tired of knocking his high hat askew. The New York Police Commissioner directed traffic from a Times Square traffic booth in a dinner jacket and boutonniere. Fifth Avenue put up bronze traffic towers. Headwaiters at the more fashionable clubs had six-figure incomes on hundred-dollar tips. Flaming Youth was the cry, and the thirty-year-olds went on a long binge which they rationalized by billing themselves as the Lost Generation. Valentino's coffin was framed in a hundred thousand dollars' worth of flowers, and such was the grief of the crowd that it drove the mounted police right through the plate-glass windows, practically on top of the corpse. Frankie Yale, a Brooklyn gangster, was shot down, and in the funeral cortege was a huge float showing a knife embedded in a bleeding heart, tastefully picked out in red and white roses, and the simple, affecting legend, "We'll see 'em, kid."

The market zoomed when a Morgan partner, on the gangplank for Europe, casually remarked that he liked General Motors. A public utility magnate had his driveway lined with highly perishable tropical flowers in the middle of the snowdrifts to receive a visiting financier, who pronounced himself charmed by the simplicity of the display. But perhaps no better illustration of the frenzy could be found than the large New York bank which offered an issue that was instantly oversubscribed for "a company and an enterprise the nature of which will be later revealed."

The tab came later; the fiddler was to be paid in blood and tears. But few will deny that while it lasted it was a marvelous tune the fiddler played. The Spanish have a saying that no one can steal the dance you've danced; the grasshopper dying in the snow may be in no position to say very much to the ant, but at least he can say that.

The twenties ended with a bang, not a whimper. It wasn't a knockout, it was a pole-axing, with dreadful lesions of body, soul, and mind and painful years of braces ahead, for the country, before learning to walk again. But it wasn't so much the hunger or the hardships of actual poverty itself that gave the haggard face of the thirties its haunted look; it was something less tangible and much worse: the universal loss of self-respect. Deprived of their function of breadwinner, men felt deeply ashamed and cruelly frustrated. Even menial jobs unworthy of a man's background and training were beyond reach. Important engineers—bridgebuilders, men who had moved mountains —pottered around their back yards, waiting for the call that never came, not daring to part with the cash a day in the city would have meant. A general cheapening and coarsening could be observed everywhere, but particularly in the big cities. In New York the debutantes who became chorines were the lucky ones; part-time prostitution was rife, and overnight the west fifties became populated by young women with cultivated accents, the residues of wardrobes of excellent tailoring, and bitter smiles of contemptuous resignation. Perhaps the greatest burden was borne by wives and mothers struggling to keep their families intact. Their biggest task was to comfort and reassure husbands whose self-confidence had been destroyed. It wasn't easy, it was often impossible; separation, divorce, and suicide shattered thousands of homes that might have withstood any number of normal crises.

The Great Depression was abnormal in its causes and in its effects. I recall a frightful art exhibit in Paris shortly after World War II showing the work of concentration-camp survivors. In picture after picture one could read a total lack of function or purpose. Instead, hopelessness and apathy, deadness of spirit and inertia of body and mind were horribly reflected. The same psychological dislocation could be found in millions of Americans in the thirties, standing silently in long queues on the streets or behind an upended crate, selling apples. . . .

But the people did not die. Like a patient after long sickness whose irritation is the first sign of recovery, a deep anger began to move in the guts of the country. The will to live began to reassert itself, slowly and not always prettily, but getting stronger all the time. It was like the rumbling in the throat of a bulldog as the hair on the back of his neck starts to rise.

An early eruption of this slow, churning anger occurred in the Midwest. A foreclosure had been ordered by the Federal Court—another in a long series of foreclosures. But this particular foreclosure was one too many, and a bristling knot of farmers came to town armed with guns. They hung a noose from the courthouse steps and dared the law to take its course. I remember reading about it and being shocked; it was rebellion, pure and simple, and the local judge, the representative of constituted authority, had been threatened and insulted. I understood the motives of the angry farmers, but I could not feel that the extremity of their behavior could be justified. I fully expected Fiorello to share my views.

"Ernest," he said on the morning that the news broke, "I want to send those farmers a message."

"Good!" I said warmly, expecting him to tell them to abide by the law, and that Congress would come to their aid.

"Take this down: 'Fight, farmers, fight. Fight for your homes and your children. Your names will live with Paul Revere's.'"

I was speechless, *dumfounded*. I wanted to protest, to say: "But people will be killed! You're inciting to riot!" But I couldn't.

Fiorello looked at me and sighed. "Never mind," he said, "I'll send it myself."

He did. There was no riot. Before long there was a moratorium on foreclosures. And once again Fiorello was on the winning side, however untenable his position may have seemed to me or anybody else at the time.

Whenever there was a crusade to fight with a good clear-cut issue to give definite form to the struggle and a lofty principle at stake, Fiorello was superb. Sometimes, though, he entered the fray after the damage had been done and was beyond correction—when further action in the matter was simply a waste of time, a beating of the proverbial dead horse. But this didn't deter Fiorello. On such occasions his eyes would glitter and he would prepare for a futile onslaught with a kind of savage relish: he had "Them" over a barrel, and even if the harm could not be undone "They" were going to suffer for it. For instance, when the Reconstruction Finance Corporation was created, $100,000,000 was voted as its capital. Almost immediately, $90,000,000 of that sum was loaned to the bank belonging to Vice President Dawes. Fiorello's temper soared like a rocket propelled by a series of time charges. With every enraged explosion he gathered altitude and momentum. But I wondered if he wasn't secretly almost happy to have been offered so vulnerable a target at which to aim his broadsides. With this in mind I was prompted to bait him a little. "I must say," I remarked as I put some papers on his desk, "your attitude about the Dawes loan seems less than statesmanlike." He bit. "How so?" I shrugged and said, "Well, in the first place the loan was necessary, and you've been in Congress long enough not to be shocked by a mere departmental favor." He seemed to shrink in his chair, but it was only to gather his forces for a spring almost literally straight up into the air. "*A departmental favor!*" he bellowed. "*Ninety million dollars,* A DEPARTMENTAL FAVOR! Get out of here!" I got out, chortling to myself. That sort of teasing was hardly sporting, but it was such fun I sometimes just couldn't resist it.

His childlike faith in the personal malevolence and unswerving evil residing in "Them" was wonderful to behold. "They" were as real to him as the Bad Giant to a child of four. "They" were ubiquitous, omniscient vultures, eager to pounce upon and devour the smallest seedling. Fiorello was ready to fight "Them" to the death, constantly on the alert lest "They" get him first. It was a convenient mythology; whenever cause and effect could not logically be deduced from a bad situation, the blame could illogically but irrefutably be thrust upon "Them." Wall Street, in the abstract, was "Their" headquarters. When a number of actual inhabitants of the Street took the stand during the Securities and Exchange Commission investigations, it must have been a cruel letdown for Fiorello. Far from being wicked or sinister, "They" turned out to be a group of very frightened and not overly bright men, some of whom had been cloth-headed enough to float hundreds of millions of dollars' worth of securities without even asking for a verified balance sheet.

There was so much unrelieved tragedy in those dark days of the early thirties that the memory tends to screen out the worst of it and admit only the drama and the occasional light moments. One such moment arose out of Fiorello's wholehearted loathing of the perfume industry. His other pet bête noire was the National Guard, which he wanted to abolish. As for perfumery, he wanted to tax the hell out of it. I knew that in connection with the current tax bill Fiorello had in mind a 13½ per cent raised excise tax on $125,000,000—this, of course, aimed directly at perfumes and other non-essential products. I also knew that it was only a question of time before he would ask me to figure out exactly what 13½ per cent of $125,-000,000 came to. So I did the obvious and worked it out ahead of time. Sure enough, he came plunging out of his office one day and said, "Ernest, work out what 13 ½ per cent of 125,000,000 is and let me know."

"Just a second," I said, and closed my eyes. "It's— $16,875,000."

He blinked. "You *sure?*"

"Sure I'm sure," I said, looking wounded.

He shook his head sadly and said humbly: "Gee, that's wonderful. I wish I could have gone to college."

I was at once stricken with remorse and confessed I had figured it out in advance, with pencil and paper, too.

He glared at me. "A wise guy!" he snorted. "Just a wise guy." He was angry, too. Which made me feel much better.

I remember getting a good deal of quiet amusement out of Fiorello's plan to insure small bank deposits. It was a good idea, something that F.D.R. was eventually to put into effect. At the time, though, Fiorello was convinced he was pioneering in a big way, and it irritated him no little when Congressman Henry Steagall, of Alabama, announced his plan to do something about protecting small deposits.

"He swiped my idea," Fiorello fumed. "Nobody ever thought of it before me."

"Nebraska tried it years ago," I observed mildly.

"Zatso?" he asked with real curiosity. "What happened?"

I sprung my little trap. "It failed."

"Oh, *well*, then. It couldn't have been anything like my idea. Mine *works*."

Quite a rat-race developed between Steagall and Fiorello to see whose bill would go in first. Steagall won, and

Fiorello was glum. I then reminded him that Brandeis was really the father of modern small-deposit insurance, having effected it successfully in Massachusetts at the turn of the century.

"Why didn't you *say* so?" he roared. "You've wasted a great deal of my time, Ernest."

As for drama, my early days with Fiorello were crammed with more of it than I could always comfortably assimilate. I can clearly remember, for instance, my sensations on the occasion of being told my first State Secret. A man's first State Secret is rather like a forbidden love affair —personal, worrisome, thrilling, and obsessively important if only in that neither can be talked about.

It happened this way: holding as he did the balance of power in Congress, Fiorello was informed about and consulted on just about everything of any conceivable importance. On this particular day the flow of high-ranking visitors into and out of his office was even heavier than usual: Federal Reserve Board members, Senate Banking Committeemen, and finally a White House courier, all of them looking ominously grave. In my sophisticated naïveté I assumed that it was simply a conclave of thirsty politicians heading for the water hole of appropriations, but I was very wrong: the situation was acute and serious.

At six-thirty that night, the last visitor departed, the inner door opened, and Fiorello motioned me in. He looked like a graven image: his jaw was set and his eyes were hard. I sat down. For a long moment he said nothing. Then: "Ernest, I am going to tell you something, and if you repeat to anyone else what I am about to say, you are going to jail—and I'll send you there. You hear?" I said yes,

I heard. "There is a run starting," he said, "a terrible run on the commercial banks."

I felt an awful chill tighten my stomach: only those who lived through those times can understand why. The nation had been wasting away economically, its strong arms withering into the long wisps of unemployment lines; but a nation-wide run on the banks was something far more horrible. It meant a paralysis of the country's nervous system, a horror so terrible that the mind balked at even considering it. I had a swift, ghastly mental picture of a cobra in a kindergarten, coiled to strike. There was no need for Fiorello to warn me not to tell anyone; I would as soon have said to a man, "You have leprosy." Fiorello saw I was suffering from shock. Like everyone else I had believed the determinedly optimistic official reports. "Good God!" I said. "What about the Federal Reserve? What's it doing? That's what it's for, for God's sake! Why don't they cover?"

"They're doing all they can," said Fiorello. "And it isn't enough. The President has called the Cabinet together." I began to see the light: emergency credit for financial institutions. "The President," continued Fiorello deliberately, "has a plan. He wants to provide for the discount of home and farm mortgages by banking institutions, the banks to get the cash on the discount."

I heaved a long sigh of relief. "Great," I said enthusiastically. "Absolutely great!"

Then, incredibly, Fiorello was saying: "No, it's not great. I'm not going to let them get away with it. They've been begging me all day—but it's no go. No dole for the millionaires. The bastards broke the People's back with their usury and now they want to unload on the Government. No," he said harshly. "No. Let them die; the People will survive."

It was too much; for the first time I lost my head in Fiorello's presence and allowed my temper to take control of my tongue. "You must be mad," I ranted. "Absolutely insane!"

He folded his arms. "Go on," he said. "Why do you think I'm insane?"

For over an hour I harangued, argued, begged, threatened, and prophesied. It was an impassioned performance. Curiously, he heard me out, even listening intently. I stated that the President's plan would avert the runs; that the discount was a virtual Governmental guarantee; that his cherished Public Housing plan would come into existence overnight on an administration departmental reform and that refinancing by further discount on new mortgages would be effected: a 4 per cent limitation, or even a 3 per cent limitation if that was what Fiorello wanted—the President would go along with that—and automatically the building industry would be pump-primed. To all of this Fiorello was impervious, waiting for me to run down. I shouted that this was more than a matter of mere economics; it was a moment of historical necessity, Jackson's Bank and Bryan's Cross of Gold rolled into one. Didn't he know the people were desperate? Did he want to finish them off? "You don't really mean what you said, do you?" I finished, gasping for breath.

"I meant every damn' word. I'm not going to let them

get away with it—palming off their lousy securities! I'd rather see the Government take over the banks outright and have done with it."

I gave up. "O.K.," I said bitterly. "Mobilize your tank corps—to kill a mouse."

He smiled grimly. "Yeah. And let me tell you something: I always get that mouse, too."

I abruptly left the office.

During the brief but deadly combat between Fiorello and the President that followed, I continued to urge the President's case. As before, Fiorello would listen attentively, but he swerved not one inch from his original position. I prepared a memorandum drawing his attention to a historical analogy involving the railroads: they had received Governmental assistance which, it seemed to me, was later proved to have been amply justified. Because I thought I had better pave the way for my composition before confronting him with it, I waited for an opportune moment. When it came I casually remarked, "Can you conceive what the economy of this country would be like without a rail system?"

"Nope."

"Do you recall the time that the railways desperately needed federal assistance?"

"Why, boy," he said scornfully, "*that* was the biggest dole the millionaires ever got. And," he added coldly, "they won't ever get another one like it, either."

Needless to say, I filed my memo in the wastebasket.

The important men abruptly stopped coming: the lines were being drawn for war. The President went ahead, as he had to, with his bill. Fiorello acted by tacking on Section 5. Section 5 provided that no mortgage would be eligible for discount, if for any reason anything more than the legal rate of interest had been paid. Fiorello knew, as did everyone else, that no mortgage could be issued without a title search and fee, and that therefore no mortgages could be discounted. Mr. Hoover could have his Bank, but it couldn't do any business. That's the way it worked out, too.

I met Fiorello at the Pennsylvania Station on his return from Washington, and he told me what had happened as we rode up in the cab. It was cold, but the inside of the cab was stifling. Fiorello had an air of grim satisfaction. Perhaps he was feeling as Andrew Jackson must have felt the night he killed Dickinson in a duel. I was thoroughly angry.

He told me that he had got Section 5 through, and then he said he had "laid back for bets." He meant, of course, that the Administration was boxed, and that it was President Hoover's move. The "bets" came quickly. The White House suggested that a Congressional Committee call for an evening conference. La Guardia was one of those receiving the invitation. "They beat around the bush all night," he chuckled, like a man who held a pat royal flush, "and about eleven o'clock the President turned to me and said, 'What about Section Five?' 'I'm not forming any rescue parties for usurers. It stays in,' I told him. Hoover didn't say anything." Apparently the President made no other overture, no suggestion for a compromise agreement, in fact pursued it no further.

But I did. "But damn it," I said, "you've burned down the barn simply to get at the rats."

"I'm getting the rats, too," said Fiorello, slumped deep in the leather seat.

"It's not *right*," I insisted, emphasizing the word by thumping the pane of the cab window with my clenched fist. Because of the cold outside and the heat inside, the glass shattered like a bomb going off, and the chill air struck us in the face. I was appalled and started to apologize, but Fiorello was delighted and cut me off, saying that he liked to see Youth back its opinions with a punch. Then, fearing that he had given me too much, he said gruffly that if I'd manage to put as much wallop into my briefs as I did into my personal opinions, we'd all be a lot better off.

I was angry and ready to go to bat again on the issue, but suddenly he had had enough of me and my ideas. When the cab stopped in front of our darkened office building, he told me to go home and relax. I walked home alone, arguing vigorously with his phantom all the way, but I knew the President's fight for mortgage discounts was lost, and it was.

The bitterest struggle, however, between the Great Engineer and the Little Flower came over the Sales Tax. It was of heroic proportions. The President's proposal was to put a tax on almost everything bought over a counter. The White House estimated that such a general tax would give the Treasury the shot in the arm it so desperately needed. Fiorello was implacably opposed. He prepared for battle like Nelson preparing for Trafalgar. He and the White House were in fundamental disagreement as to how to get the Ship of State off the rocks onto which it had foundered in the fall of 1929. Fiorello's theory, which was substantially the same as Roosevelt's two years later, called for floating the ship by working from the keel up and not from the superstructure down. Both Fiorello and F.D.R. believed that finance at the lowest levels meant the top levels would ultimately prosper. In the raging financial hurricane, Fiorello boiled down his course to the repeated slogan "No dole for the millionaires." The economic seas could boil and the winds of bankruptcy blow Beaufort's scale itself out of the Pilot House, but Fiorello stood on the bridge like an immovable block of black basalt; *"No dole for the millionaires!"*

A White House conference of Congressional leaders was called. To this one, Fiorello was *not* invited. President Hoover appealed to both parties to support a Sales Tax. The Democrats needed next to no persuading. John Nance Garner, in fact, volunteered to lead the Administration program from the Floor, which he proceeded to do, calling the tax "not a Republican, not a Democratic, but an American tax." The Republican Congressmen, of course, were more than willing to follow the President.

Over four hundred Congressmen were aligned with the White House and only five were not, but one of those five was Fiorello H. La Guardia. As I recall it, the bill was slated for vote on a Thursday. Garner made his speech and was cheered to the echo. But Fiorello, the master parliamentarian, succeeded in introducing a technicality which forced the vote over until the following Tuesday. He had ground the "enemy" to a pause, if not a halt; and now he went to work. He splashed headlines across the nation, trumpeting that it was a matter of national shame that people who had not enough to eat should be forced to pay a tax on what little bread they could buy; he charged that underfed babies in the crib were being taxed of the strong bodies they could never have. He really laid it on. Editorially, the press, particularly in the Midwest, took him severely to task. One called him "an alien with an alien mind, a foreign interloper." He asked me to get him a copy. I did. He cut it out, and put it in his wallet.

Knowing he was going to make a speech, I went furiously to work over the week end on a study of sales taxes as failures in other countries. Canada, after her first high hopes, had had a particularly rough experience with it, and on that I based my thesis that in a North American democracy a sales tax just couldn't work. I buttressed the argument at every point I could, and when I brought it in to Fiorello I felt that it was pretty well mortised and tenoned. It was on legal-sized lined yellow paper. I stood slightly to the side and behind him when he put on his glasses and started to read. I read over his shoulder, trying to see it through his eyes. He finished the first page, and then with the daintiest of gestures held it over the wastebasket and let it flutter in. Not a word was spoken. The second sheet followed the first. So did the third. The rest he handed back to me unread, without a word.

I wasn't embarrassed. I was just beside myself with anxiety for him. I felt he was walking toward battle unarmed. "What *are* you going to say, Major?" I asked.

"I am going to say," said Fiorello with level deliberation, "*soak the rich!*" My emotional viscera collapsed like a house of cards. I thought it was a terrible thing to say, utterly undignified and a hardly adequate response to a

noble call like "an American tax." I just walked outside
and sat down.

But I was young and inexperienced. Perhaps I didn't
think much of Fiorello's approach, but a great many Congressmen seemed to. Over the week end, Fiorello's ranks
started to swell. He was almost as oblivious to this as to
the make-up of his opposition. He smiled when the tele-
grams of support came in, but all he said was, "Their con-
sciences are catching up with them."

The "enemy's" lines started to crack, and finally they
avalanched. Fiorello told me that he had had a call from
Jack Garner, whom he enormously liked and respected.
"He seemed quite broken up." Fiorello laughed. "He said,
'Florio'—he always calls me Florio—'I've changed my
mind. You can quote me as being against the Sales Tax,
and I'll stand by anything you say.' "

On Tuesday the House reconvened. Fiorello's floor vote
showdown approached. The "soak the rich" tag still stuck
in my craw. He just couldn't, I felt, make such a raw
statement. I took a crack at writing a policy approach, an
almost blanket appropriation of some of Webster's, Lincoln's and Brandeis' nobler sentiments. I should have
known better: Fiorello hated quotes, and hated para-
phrases of quotes even more.

He patiently read it, however, without throwing it in
the basket this time. When he finished, he said, "Yeah."

"Yeah, what?" I asked.

"Yeah, nothing," he said. "I'll say it my way."

"Which is?" I flinched, waiting to hear the dreadful
phrase fall like a Mosler safe dropping seven stories, but

hoping against hope it wouldn't. But it did: "*Soak the Rich!*" he bellowed.

I had the hopeless feeling of being on the back seat of a toboggan at the start of a run. "Major," I said earnestly, "you are *sure* to be misunderstood."

He squinted his eyes at me defiantly. "So was Christ," he murmured.

Of course he won, hands down. The House reversed itself. The Administration suffered a terrible defeat, a defeat so great that it never could rally the Congress thereafter.

Long afterward, Fiorello was reminiscing: "They put Baruch alongside of me on the Congressional that Friday," he said, "and he talked my ear off all the way up. Boy, They really wanted that Sales Tax." He chuckled maliciously. "But They didn't get it. I showed Them!"

V

"They" answered to a variety of definitions in Fiorello's lexicon, but the common denominator that obtained in all cases was summed up in the one word "exploitation." Whoever exploited his fellow men was one of "Them," and as such deserved to be dealt with as St. George dealt with the Dragon. Whether Fiorello loved St. George more than he hated the Dragon I was never able to determine, but I do know that if he was unable to thrust home the sword to the Dragon's heart, he was content, for the time being, to give it a few swift kicks in the shin. When it seemed to him that the circumstances warranted it, he was capable of vindictiveness and cruelty. I once tentatively offered the gratuitous information that I could understand and approve of hard tackling and brutal punishment; that so long as the rules of the game weren't violated I would not hesitate to fracture both of a ball carrier's legs. But, I added sanctimoniously, I drew the line at gouging or biting at the bottom of a scrimmage pile. Fiorello was unimpressed. "Yeah, sure," he said, "that's fine." But I had missed the point—or rather, *his* point: it wasn't a foot-

47

ball game to him and he wasn't bound by any official rules. When he fought, he fought to win because he *had* to win; he would lose more than the goalposts if he lost. Specifically, his defeat would mean the defeat of thousands of other people, victims of exploitation by some one wicked individual or a small group of evil men.

He firmly believed that such men were motivated solely by Greed, that Greed begat Poverty, and Poverty, Evil—these in capital letters, always. He never doubted the existence of these Bad Men—he had seen and suffered their handiwork, he said—and he was bent on their extermination. They had sold tainted beef to the Army during the Spanish-American War, and he held them directly accountable for the death of his father. Time and again he swore that he would have such criminal negligence in time of war made a capital offense. Only he didn't call it negligence, he called it murder. Significantly, his very first act as a Congressman was to submit a bill calling for the death penalty for those who knowingly sold faulty goods to the armed services in time of war. He called it murder, too, when he referred to the Italian airplane companies who had sold aircraft to the U. S. Army which they knew to be defective—planes their own test pilots had been killed in. And he was no less outspoken about the domestic manufacturers of the infamous Liberty motors. Everyone knew that they were substandard, but everyone also knew that almost none of them were used. I was willing to go along with an indictment for graft, but not for murder. To Fiorello's way of thinking, however, it was a simple case of black and white.

At the top of his hierarchy of iniquity the bankers

roosted, like foul birds of prey. In Fiorello's mind they were forever behind huge mahogany desks in vast, vault-like offices, scheming. The Panic of 1893 was a typical case in point, he stated. Here was that fine President, Cleveland, sweating it out in the White House, and there was Mr. Morgan, holed up in a luxurious Washington hotel and sending word to the President that he would bail him out whenever the signal was given—at a 10 per cent profit. Why, it was enough to make a man's blood boil; and, more than forty years after the event, Fiorello's did. Cleveland at first rebuffed the financier, but Morgan had powerful friends who were also part of the Conspiracy, and in the end the President had to knuckle under.

Fiorello's knowledge of American history was encyclopedic, but his deductions were sometimes startling. Alexander Hamilton was the villain of our national infancy: look what he did with the Continental currency, redeeming it at par, and he himself in on the deal. Henry Clay wasn't much better, and Daniel Webster was often paid hard cash for much of the legislation he introduced. ("Didn't you know that, Ernest? What are they *teaching* in the colleges these days?") He began a speech I heard one night with the words, "I have changed my opinion of bankers." I nearly fell off my chair. But I shouldn't have batted an eye, because, "Yes," he continued, "once I admired and respected them." If so, he must have been in knee-pants at the time. It certainly wasn't at any time I knew him.

Not far below the bankers came the monopolies, which Fiorello regarded as secret taxing combinations levying hidden interest imposts on the people. According to him, they did not hesitate to corrupt high Government officials.

He knew the inside story of the railroad scandals of the eighties to the smallest detail. The "Power Trust" (this was before the Holding Company Act) was a sinister, voracious beast feeding on the vitals of the public. He abominated the lobbyists who served it, reserving for them some of the strongest language I ever heard him utter: "public-utility whores" was one of his milder epithets. Once he was invited to a gathering of other Congressmen at the Mayflower. Generally speaking he led a monk's life in Washington, staying at home and, among other things, reading *every* bill that came before his Committees, but this invitation he accepted. He was raising his first highball to his lips when a colleague quipped, "Look out, Fiorello, the Power Trust is paying for that drink!" Without a word he put the glass down and walked out.

Judges and lawyers were next in line for his disdain. For the great jurists he had, of course, immense respect, but the run-of-the-mill judiciary he conceived to be incompetent holders of sinecures which in many cases they had bought, one way or another. When the Astor Estate applied to the Courts for relief from an $8,000,000 inheritance tax, Fiorello jumped into the middle of the fray by questioning whether the tax dollars shouldn't be used to battle the depression. And for good insulting measure he questioned the worth of the Astor heirs to the community. I urged a more temperate line; after all, the case was before the courts and ought not to be commented on. "I damn' well intend to comment on it before they make away with the boodle!" But, I objected, he was giving the impression that he was attacking the integrity of the Bench. "Exactly what I *am* doing, my boy!" he retorted.

Captain La Guardia in World War I

Politician . . .

. . . and Legislator

Champion of young and old

Another victory

United Press

Bad news in Harlem

Press conference on the race riots

"Ernest" today

The Astor application was granted, and Fiorello sent off a stinging letter to the Judiciary Committee. He raised such an unholy row that Congress began to pay attention to his contention that an end should be put to the practice of "allowing dead men to control the nation's finances." Just what direct effect all this brouhaha had on the Supreme Court is hard to say, but the fact remains that shortly thereafter the Supreme Court held that the taxing power of the United States was not restricted to purposes of revenue, and from that moment inheritance taxes were doubled and redoubled. Foundations sprouted like mushrooms, but the backbone of family control was broken. History will ultimately determine the merits of the matter, but meanwhile a significant economic pattern in American life had been decisively broken.

The day came when Fiorello was to demand an audit of judges' expense accounts while on circuit. I heard he was personally checking over no less than twenty-nine, one of which listed expenses totalling $2,500 for a three-day stay in a neighboring state. At that time $2,500 was a very respectable sum of money, and there was considerable speculation as to the tastes and personal habits of this ornament of the Bench.

Corporation lawyers were, to Fiorello, the worst of their breed. They too inspired uncommonly strong language, such as "pimps for Wall Street." There was, to be sure, a stench emanating from bankruptcy and receivership cases, but Fiorello seldom gave the Bar associations much credit for their earnest attempts to clean house. When in Philadelphia an involved witness excused himself from the stand, went to the men's room, and there slashed his throat,

Fiorello's only reaction was a harsh grunt. I wondered if it was bravado—if, like me, he didn't really feel some sympathy for a desperate, cornered man forced to the point of taking his life in a public toilet. But Fiorello, as I said, was playing for keeps; whatever he may have felt, all he could afford to show was an air of grim satisfaction.

The ostentations of the very wealthy were to Fiorello what banderillas are to the bull. He described to me in tones of incredulity and indignation the lavish appointments of a huge country club maintained by Andrew Mellon outside Pittsburgh. He patently expected me to share his moral outrage, as though the mere recitation of such indecencies as golf courses, tennis courts, and stables should have me reaching for the gun over the fireplace. I managed a few feeble shakes of the head, but all I could think was that if Fiorello planned to make his anger public we would never, never be invited to this wonderful place. Finally he exploded, "Well, don't you agree?" I tried to explain that whereas I would be glad to slug it out when it was a question of a real social injustice, it didn't actually seem to me important whether a rich man owned one or twenty private clubs. Far more important issues were at stake. After all, I temporized, the fight was for the bridge and the wheel; who cared about the satined cabins below? I braced myself for the blast. Instead, he drew back and examined me with doubtful and concerned eyes, as though he had just heard me say I was the victim of some mental infirmity. He patted me briefly on the shoulder and withdrew into his office without a word.

Possessions, as such, were of no interest to Fiorello. He felt it was easy for a man to become enslaved by his pos-

sessions, to become the victim of his own greed. His in-
difference to the usual hallmarks of "gracious living" extended to very small things. One Christmas, for instance,
all of us in the office agreed that the ideal gift for him
would be an expensive, flame-grained Kaywoodie to take
the place of his cheap, evil-smelling corncob. He was indeed very touched by the present and by our presentation
of it. He said it was something he had always wanted: we
shouldn't have done it. He was quite right: we shouldn't.
Within a few days the horrible old corncob was smoldering
away again and the handsome Kaywoodie lay in its felt case
gathering dust.

Money in more than adequate amounts meant absolutely nothing to him. "Do you know who the wealthiest
man in the world is?" he asked me once. I shook my head.
"Gandhi. The only thing he owns is a sheet, and nobody
would think of depriving him of it."

It was inevitable, I suppose, that Fiorello single out
some one person on whom to concentrate the ferocity of
his vast displeasure. And, because of all he symbolized,
I suppose it was natural that Treasury Secretary Andrew
Mellon should be the man selected.

Andrew Mellon and Fiorello H. La Guardia were at
opposite poles of the American political world. Mellon
was a small, wispy man with the appearance of a medieval
ascetic. His manner was precise and aloof, cold as the great
steel state which he ruled; Fiorello, warm and mercurial,
was his perfect foil. As far as Fiorello was concerned, Mellon was Privilege personified. He considered his clash with
Mellon as a battle between the champions of two opposing
forces: the spiritual sovereignty of the People and the ma-

terial power of the Industrial Barons. He amassed a formidable dossier on Mellon, never to be tested in a court of law. Mellon for his part regarded Fiorello's antagonism as the turgid, unreasoning voice of the masses against his class. Fiorello never doubted that Mellon, through his dummies, was guilty of violating the law on any number of counts, and in making his charges he was confident that he had "the goods" on his adversary.

Late one afternoon Fiorello sent for me. "I'm going to impeach Mellon," he announced. "Get me a brief."

"It would help if you'd tell me what grounds you have for an impeachment, Major," I said.

"There's a statute that forbids the Secretary of the Treasury's being a director of any private corporation. Mellon controls the Aluminum Corporation of the United States and Canada. That's a fact. Now get the exact law and base your brief on it."

I had a fleeting picture of batteries of distinguished counsel on the top floors of Pittsburgh office buildings, of the old foxes of the New York Bar downtown, of the formidable resources everywhere that comprised the Mellon Empire—all of them pitted against me and my little brief —me, a young squirt not yet even admitted to the Bar. It would take months to prepare a case that wouldn't be ripped to pieces like a pack of wildcats playing with a silk handkerchief.

"When do you want this?" I asked.

"No rush," he said. "Any time tomorrow morning. I'm blasting at noon."

I made a wild dash for the Law Library and went frantically to work. It soon became apparent to me that there was no case against Mellon at all. Stock ownership wasn't the same as directorship, and that was that. And since the action was criminal in nature, the law had to be strictly construed. Fiorello was out of luck. I did, however, uncover a case in which a Secretary of War, Belton, to be exact, had been impeached for ownership in an Indian trading post doing business with the War Department. It wasn't much, but it was all I could find.

I hurried back to the office and explained to Fiorello the nice distinction between owning stock and being a director, but he brushed aside this piffling bit of legalistic hairsplitting. He said that Mellon controlled the directors, who were just dummies, so it was the same thing. I began to object that it *wasn't* the same thing, but he sawed his hand through the air impatiently, indicating he'd heard enough on that score. "What else?" he snapped. I told him about Belton's troubles over the Indian trading post. He was disgusted with it and with me, and said so. He advised me to get back to the Library and unearth something with a bit more meat on the bone. So back I went and stayed until closing time without finding a thing. Then I trudged home.

I hadn't been asleep very long when the phone went off. "Ernest," shrilled Fiorello in my ear, "tell me more about those God-damned Indians of yours."

"Not mine," I corrected, "Belton's. Well—" I went into the details. When I finished he seemed satisfied, even pleased.

"Fine," he said.

"But it's not a case," I warned.

"You leave that to me," he said, and hung up.

Several days went by before Fiorello began shelling Mellon in Washington, demanding his immediate impeachment. He was firing for effect, but it seemed to me he had nothing in his arsenal but duds. The fact remains, however, that a few days later President Hoover appointed Mellon Ambassador to England.

The next time I saw Fiorello he was merry as a grig. "Well," he gloated, "I got him."

"The law wasn't on your side, though," I said.

"Oh, yes it was," he beamed. "The Law of Reciprocal Damage."

Personally, I failed to see the reason for Fiorello's glee; it didn't seem to me that Mellon had suffered much. At least, I had never heard that being appointed Ambassador to the Court of St. James's was tantamount to being seated on the wrong side of Lindy's. Fiorello, though, oozed gratification—until the day the papers carried a picture of Mellon in knee breeches. Fiorello was beside himself: "Look at that, will you? Just *look* at that! It's—it's un-American!"

"It's what?" I asked.

Well, knee breeches weren't in the American tradition, he grumbled.

I pointed out that George Washington was seldom pictured in anything else, and was told I was a Wise Guy.

Like most good haters, Fiorello had a huge compensatory capacity for love. His devotion to his country, for instance, was wholehearted and profound, without a trace of that fatuity so often present in public figures. He deeply loved the American experience as a whole. His patriotism was unforced and built-in, as much a part of him as his lungs and liver. He never, to my knowledge, used it as a tool; it meant too much to him for that. "The Republic" was no mere catch phrase—it was an article of faith. The great leaders of the Republic whom he venerated above all others were Jefferson, Jackson, and Lincoln. In the second flight he placed Theodore Roosevelt, Grover Cleveland, and Woodrow Wilson. Whenever he talked about these heroes of his I was always struck by the simon-purity of his humility—and it wasn't often that I was inclined to think of Fiorello as a humble man.

His respect and affection for Congress were equally real, but at times I had trouble keeping a straight face. It was the fashion, sparked by Will Rogers, to poke fun at Congress. Fiorello was not amused. He even hinted darkly that "They" were behind the lampooning, intent on discrediting Congress in the eyes of the people. Congress was his fraternity—indeed, his alma mater—and his loyalty to it reminded me of an Old Blue reminiscing in his club bar.

"The People" was a magic phrase with Fiorello. Whenever he used it, one could almost hear a military band playing "The Battle Hymn of the Republic" in the middle distance. It was a grand image, a Promethean symbol. I think it was Bertrand Russell who said that the principal fallacy of the twentieth century was what he termed the Theory of the Superior Virtue of the Oppressed. It was a theory, however, to which Fiorello subscribed without reservation. The People, in his mind, were the masses of downtrodden, noble poor who desperately needed his help. This was understandable: a Congressman's office in those days was an ideal laboratory for the study of human misery. There was more concentrated suffering and despair in our anteroom than in an emergency ward on a snowy New Year's Eve. Small wonder, then, that when Fiorello said, "The People," he had in mind not the descendants of Minute Men, pioneers, and empire-builders, but a wretched huddle of lost souls in distress. He was their faithful servant, but he did not think they were very bright. He no more expected them to help themselves than the Arthurian knight expected the fair maiden to descend from her tower and join him in routing the wicked Baron who had imprisoned her.

Though Fiorello enjoyed, I'm sure, the role of protector and the sensation of being needed, I do not believe he had in his make-up any of the martyr's special brand of vanity. His view of "The People" may have been artificially conditioned by circumstance and his own ego, but *people*—hundreds of thousands of them—were very badly off indeed, and his heart bled for them. Their suffering he considered a personal affront, and he consecrated himself to its alleviation. We passed Union Square in a cab early one autumn evening, and as we waited for a light we could catch snatches of an impassioned harangue by a sleazy-looking, wild-eyed soapbox orator. "Listen to that poor idiot," Fiorello muttered. Then he sighed heavily and added, "The hell of it is, he's right."

No, he may have sentimentalized the concept of "The People," but he did not sentimentalize their suffering. He had grown up in the dreadful days of the sweatshop. Women in Lower East Side tenements worked at their sewing machines 72 hours a week and earned less than $5.00 for it. He had seen women in picket lines beaten and hauled off to jail. He said he had once joined a picket line himself, but in spite of his best efforts he couldn't get himself arrested as a test case. He told me about employers introducing gangsters into their shop to maintain order, and collecting 30 per cent on their investments with the full knowledge that their workers, undernourished and inadequately housed, were dying of tuberculosis. They were murderers in his eyes, mass murderers, and their profits were blood money. At an early age Fiorello decided to do something about it. What he did is a matter of record. Few names shine brighter than his in the annals of social reform: wages and hours legislation, health regulation, factory reform and slum clearance—these and many other enlightened steps were given shape and momentum by Fiorello La Guardia in his role of Defender of The People.

The term "Children," used collectively, was an even more sacred symbol to Fiorello than "The People." I remember an occasion when he kept several important people from the Federal Reserve waiting for most of a whole afternoon while he discussed the future of a crippled ten-year-old with the boy's parents. The Federal Reserve matter was important and his decision with regard to it was crucial, but it was not as important to Fiorello's way of thinking as the problems raised by this handicapped child. The boy had been run over by a trolley, I remember. Fiorello had punched through a private bill for $10,-000 compensation. Now he wanted to make certain that the boy himself would benefit by the money. It was a poor family, and the temptation to spend it in other ways would be overwhelming. Fiorello told the parents that their son had to be specially educated, that his disability would make it impossible for him to become a carpenter or a plumber or a truck driver. He wanted the boy to be a teacher. He explained his reasoning again and again to them, to make sure they understood. He was by turns patient and kindly, stern and dictatorial. I was reminded of Daniel Webster's famous plea for the woodchuck's life. After he finally let them go he turned to me and said: "They're good people. But dumb. You have to keep telling them."

On the subject of child labor, Fiorello was rabid. He didn't regard it as a problem; it was a sacrilege. He was absolutely tireless in his determination to stamp it out. He hated it with a fanatic's intensity, and in fact one could almost hear in his tirades on the subject the very accents of John Brown denouncing slavery and prophesying doom for the country that could tolerate so heinous a sin. And of course child labor was a sin. Eight-year-old girls worked ten-hour shifts in cotton mills; the Breaker Boys turned in twelve hours a day at the mines. It seemed incredible to both of us that such things could happen here; and no less incredible that so many stumbling blocks were placed in the path of legislation that would eventually end the evil.

His love of children in general attached itself to the particular. Once, the police of a certain Western state were accused of unnecessary roughness in their handling of a kidnaper. According to some news stories they had worked him over with a baseball bat. When I called the incident to Fiorello's attention, he ground his teeth and said savagely, "They should have put spikes in the bat first, and beaten the son of a bitch to death."

Part of Fiorello's boyhood had been spent at an Army post in Arizona, and he told me about the way the Indians had been treated by incompetent and dishonest political hacks sent out by the Government. These characters simply put the Indian Reservation money in their pockets and fed the chief a line of threats involving personal reprisal if he uttered a word of protest to Washington. As a result, the Indians literally did not have enough to eat. The wives of enlisted men used to feed Indian children from their own none too ample stores, but it wasn't nearly enough. "How would you like to have seen a playmate of yours go hungry? What would you have thought about the men who stole food out of children's mouths?" There was nothing theatrical about his anger as he said this. It was simply that one of his great loves, Children, had been victimized by one of his great hates, Exploitation.

Fiorello's fondness for Eskimos exemplifies the pattern beautifully: they were susceptible to exploitation; they were not very smart; they needed a vigorous champion to protect their rights; they were touchingly childlike creatures. Fiorello took up the cudgels on their behalf with a will. Before long "La Guardia's damn' Eskimos" was a by-word in Congress. A joke went the rounds to the effect that after Fiorello had obtained certain benefits for a tribe of nomad Eskimos somewhere north of Point Barrow, the Department of the Interior couldn't find them to make the benefits available. Fiorello chuckled. "That just shows," he said, "how neglected they've been. They can't even be found!"

The longer I worked with Fiorello, and the better I knew him, the clearer the pattern became: his instinctive mistrust and dislike of the Haves and his instinctive compassion for and identification with the Have Nots. Sympathy for the underdog is a much advertised national characteristic; it was, I believe, the cornerstone of Fiorello's character. But whereas so many people are content to sympathize and let it go at that, Fiorello translated his warm indignation into positive and constructive action. It was no less, he felt, than his plain duty—and destiny—to do so.

VI

Fiorello had very little use for royalty. He couldn't understand why they wouldn't admit they were anachronisms and just clear out. Instead, he said, they hung around, waiting to be kicked out, useless and outmoded. He called them loafers. An incident that occurred while he was American Consul at Trieste before World War I typified his attitude toward the titled aristocracy. The Austrian Court requested that a liner with nearly a thousand immigrants aboard be held in port a couple of extra days so that it might be visited by the Archduchess of Austria and the Royal Household. The immigrants were expected to remain in the swelter below decks while the inspection was going on. Fiorello said, in effect, to hell with the Archduchess. "Imagine," he said to me, "keeping those poor women and children shut away from the fresh air. They might have gotten very sick." The liner sailed on schedule, and the royal inspection was called off. "They kicked me out of the State Department for that," he added, "but it was worth it."

Bookmakers irritated him, too, though for different reasons. They battened on a human weakness. He had a scheme, though, for ruining bookmaking once for all. Everybody should bet; those who won would insist on being paid off, and those who lost should refuse to pay up. "That'd fix 'em," he said. But he admitted the idea, if inspired, was impractical.

Notwithstanding his basic attitude or his later drive on bookmakers, however, Fiorello in 1931 was not averse to putting an occasional two bucks down on a horse. Not only that, he boasted that he was psychic; he could pick long shots. "It's part system, and part intuition," he would say. I pressed him for details, but he wasn't talking. I knew, though, who was placing his bets for him: Louie Espresso, the Republican leader down in the Village. Louie knew a bookie who took two-dollar bets. My curiosity was sufficiently aroused for me to drop over once to see him. We talked about a lot of things, mostly Fiorello, before I introduced the subject of betting. In another connection we had just agreed that Fiorello was the most intuitive man either of us had ever known, and now I remarked that he had told me his intuition enabled him to pick long-shot horses. At this, Louie sniffed; he said Fiorello was talking through his fedora. "He's got a system?" he snorted. "Some system! You know what he does? He bets on Italian jockeys, and then only once in a blue moon; and if they don't come in he screams like a baby. Coltiletti," said Louie sarcastically, "has a big run. So Fiorello's happy as a lark. *Now* Fiorello's an expert. Next time?" Louie opened his hands expressively and shrugged. "And when they don't come in," he finished indignantly, "he blames me—and I never bet on the damned things."

It annoyed Fiorello that gambling debts were referred

to as debts of honor. "Here is a boob," he would say, "with kids that are hungry. Does he use his last two bucks to buy them food? No. This boob pays it over to some tinhorn bookie because his honor—his *honor*, if you please —is involved. Huh! Some honor. Some boob." Professional gamblers he disapproved of, not because he objected to gambling, provided you could afford it, but because they made a habit of corrupting public officials.

Besides gamblers, bookies, and royalty, Fiorello harbored a good many other minor antipathies: he disdained Big Brass that acted like Big Brass; he frowned upon pool hall proprietors; and male ballet dancers made him fidget. He was quick to notice and deride anything unusual or "foppish" in men's attire. One time I had some trouble with an ankle which had been broken years before and which always stiffened up when the weather was raw; probably somebody had kicked it in passing in the subway during rush hour. Anyway, it had to be kept warm. Because I never could stand wool next to my skin, I taped a surgical compress over it and concealed it by wearing a pair of spats. Fiorello was scandalized when he saw them. He stared at them for a long moment and then glowered at me over his glasses. "Your underwear's showing," he remarked. I explained. He snorted, indicating that it would take more than a broken ankle, or a broken neck, for that matter, to get *him* to wear spats.

He loved music, and consequently was partial to all musicians. In every other area of creativity, however, a good artist to Fiorello was a guy who got paid well for his work. To painting he was generally indifferent, though he liked representational sculpture. Abstracts of any kind made him impatient. I once mentioned the name of a friend of mine, an abstract painter who in my opinion was doing fine work. Fiorello humphed. "Never heard of him."

"So what?"

"So take my sculptor friend Piccirili," he said. "He makes plenty of money sculpting."

"What's that got to do with Art?"

"Not much, maybe, but it's got a lot to do with the artist."

Poetry left him utterly cold, and fiction was of no particular interest to him. He astonished me once, however, by referring to Fannie Hurst, whom both he and Mrs. La Guardia knew well, as not only a great woman but a great writer. I allowed as how he ought to employ that adjective with a bit more discrimination. "Not only is she a great writer," he continued, as though I had not spoken, "but she has tremendous character. She went on a diet and stuck to it, which is something you should think about doing soon."

I suppose his contempt for pool halls arose from his conviction that time was precious and ought not to be idled away. I doubt that he had any hobbies, as the term is generally understood. He must have belonged to a great many clubs, but he never spent any time with them during the time I worked for him. There was one club to which he had apparently belonged for many years and which he always referred to with affection. It was called, of all things, the Tough Club, and its headquarters were down in the Village. I often tried to get him to tell me about it, but he wouldn't. He took his membership in the Masons seriously enough, it seemed to me, and whenever he mentioned that organization it was with obvious respect. I surprised him one afternoon in the act of executing a pretty tricky step in what appeared to be a spirited clog dance. If I had walked in to find the Archbishop of Canterbury bobbing for apples I couldn't have been more astonished. He retreated hastily behind his desk and began fiddling with papers. I begged him to go on, not to let me stop him. He refused. I asked him where in the world he had learned anything like that, and he replied grumpily that he and Ferdie Pecora had once been end men in a minstrel show at the Elks. And in future he would thank me to knock before I came blundering in.

Fiorello seldom discussed Churches. He was an Episcopalian, but my impression is that he did not often attend services. He carried on a considerable correspondence with clergymen, however, and spoke warmly to me of the Methodist ministers who held meetings in Pennsylvania to which the miners were attracted. Had they assembled except under the aegis of the clergy, they would have been clubbed in the company towns, Fiorello said. His relations with the ministry were correct and careful, and in the cases of certain individual ministers, cordial. But he did not hesitate to fight for repeal of the Eighteenth Amendment even though the Methodist and Baptist churches were strongly pro-Prohibition. I believe he favored Planned Parenthood, otherwise known as Birth Control. At least, he said on one occasion that what the world needed was fewer and better babies. Once during the depression a very poor man entered one of the fashionable Fifth Avenue churches and killed himself there by taking poison. The Church Board issued a statement, which looked very callous in print, to the effect that the deceased man was not a member of the congregation. Fiorello handed it to me to read. I said, "The poor man." Scathingly, Fiorello said, "The poor church."

Fiorello had no more idiosyncrasies than the next man—or rather, the next great man—but he was dogged about them. He saw nothing funny in them. The ability to laugh at himself was one of the few gifts that had been denied him. As a consequence, though he was not a vain man, the few things that did touch his vanity brooked no impertinence, and as a consequence of *that* I found myself unable to resist teasing him on those very points. He liked, for instance, to think of himself as a prophet. Not only could he read the handwriting on the wall; he claimed it as his own script. He would thunder like a Jeremiah against iniquity, intermingling grave warnings and terrible threats. I was often called upon to bear witness, after some dire event, that he had warned of the imminence of the catastrophe. Cassandra was no more certain of her powers of foretelling the future than Fiorello. It honestly awed him, this uncanny faculty of his. Maliciously, I observed that Al Smith had it too. (Consciously or unconsciously, Fiorello considered Al Smith one of his few real rivals, and I never hesitated to take full advantage of that knowledge.)

"What d'ya mean?" Fiorello said crossly. "What did he ever predict?"

"All the most significant social reforms," I replied. "Ask any reporter."

"Oh, reforms," sneered Fiorello. "That long-range stuff

is easy. Tell those reporters of yours to ask him what's going to happen three weeks from now."

Fiorello's "gift" for prophecy was a logical by-product of his vast self-confidence in general. There was almost literally no situation that Fiorello did not feel himself the master of, no problem so knotty but that he could not disentangle it, given a minute or two of concentrated thought. He had answers to everything. I remember one evening, at the little speak we sometimes frequented, our talking about the Chinese tong wars that had raged while I had been a reporter on the *News*. I repeated a story one of the boys had told me about a triple killing over a Chinese restaurant in Brooklyn. If it didn't have a twist of humor, I said, it certainly illustrated Oriental fatalism. It appeared that two On Leong Tong hatchetmen had gone up the back-stairs to a Hip Sing kitchen and, actually using hatchets, had killed two cooks by hacking their heads. Then the On Leongs ran out through the restaurant, but in the getaway one had been shot and killed by a Hip Sing. The place was a shambles when the reporters arrived from headquarters together with the Homicide Squad and the Assistant D.A. The place was awash with blood and tables were overturned—complete disorder. "What happened?" they breathlessly asked the proprietor. Pointing at the awful scene, he said sadly, "Everybody ran out without paying the check."

Fiorello smiled his wan smile of the not very amused, so I decided to develop the horror as opposed to the humorous side of the tong wars. I said that five Hip Sings with floppy black hats came out on the stage of a Chinese theater one night and opened fire on the On Leong audience. It was terrible, ghastly, I had heard.

Here Fiorello broke in. "Listen," he said derisively, "Don't you know how to stop a tong war?"

"No," I said. "Do *you* know how to stop a tong war?"

"Sure," he said. "Don't you really know?" He repeated, as if I might be pretending ignorance of something which *everybody* knew, the way every Boy Scout knows how to apply a tourniquet. That simple. It nearly was.

"Why," said Fiorello, "you just stage sweeping immigration raids until they quit. They quit right away, because half of them are here illegally, smuggled in. In fact, they never start acting up if they know that raids will follow. It's easy."

His confidence in his own resources often led him to make outrageous shots in the dark, and it always irritated me to see how lucky he usually was. Once, for example, a large manufacturer out in Queens issued a public statement bitterly criticizing him. Fiorello had never heard of the concern before. I know, because he asked me who they were. I didn't know, so he just went ahead and dictated an answering statement saying that he welcomed attack from an organization which was so notorious in the bad treatment of its employees. I was staggered by this and asked him how he knew this firm was hard on its employees. He simply admitted he didn't know the first thing about the firm, but he said he knew because *everybody* was bad to their employees, except him of course, and he forthwith issued the statement. I was confounded when some of the firm's employees communicated with him and said they were glad he was fighting their battle. As I recall, a committee came over, and Fiorello acted grave and thoughtful, nodding as if he had been aware of their grievances for a long time. He got off a second barrage, and I heard nothing further about the matter.

But the very apogee, the ultimate in good luck, was illustrated by an incident that had occurred some years before, and which he told me about with a devilish kind of glee. Bill Dwyer, the town's biggest bootlegger, had been given a dinner on top of the Biltmore Hotel by the very best people in town on the occasion of something social connected with race tracks. Some bright lads got the idea of bringing over a few field artillery horses from Governors Island in honor of the occasion, and they were duly transported to the Biltmore Roof. The publicity was great—until Fiorello's eye lit upon the pictures. That gave him a chance to ask a number of cruel, logical questions to which there were no logical answers.

"What," Fiorello telegraphed the Secretary of War, "were Field Artillery horses doing on the Biltmore Roof?" No one in the War Department knew, of course. The whole thing was ridiculous. Very well, if no one knew what those horses were doing on the Roof, since when was the Field Artillery called out to honor bootleggers? No one knew the answer to that one either.

Fiorello had a fine week, savoring the situation the way a connoisseur would relish a magnificent Amontillado. What about the City Elevator Inspection for safety? How many horses had been allowed in an elevator? He could find no provisions in the City Code. All questions were telegraphed to the proper authorities. But what authority has jurisdiction over horses in elevators? He conducted a search on it. No one knew. He caught any number of people off base, and he loved it. And why *not?* It isn't often that a reform politician can ask what horses—and U.S. Government horses at that—are doing on top of a sky-scraper!

His luck didn't always hold, however. At one point during my stint with Fiorello, a man named Carl G. Fisher was trying to build up Montauk Point as a prosperous resort. Fisher had had an impressive record in building up Miami, and he was trying to do the same for the eastern tip of Long Island. Fiorello came in one day in a towering rage, saying that Fisher had got some of the Fleet detailed to Montauk Point for summer exercises. Also involved was the Navy Band. Fiorello said that was very hard on the enlisted men; besides, what the hell was the U.S. Navy doing, helping to promote a real-estate development? He got Congressman Fred Britten, of Illinois, a member of the Naval Affairs Committee, on the telephone and threw a fit. He demanded an investigation, but got nowhere with Britten. Off went a telegram to Secretary of the Navy Charles F. Adams. I had misgivings; Secretary Adams was a cool, correct New Englander who wasn't likely to be very far off base.

"Under just what section of the Navy Law has the Navy Band been authorized to play at Montauk Point?" was Fiorello's belligerent wired inquiry.

"Section X. Yours, Adams," was the immediate reply. Backfire. I looked up the Section. The authority was there, all right.

The fiasco was all the more galling to Fiorello because he prided himself—with complete justice—on his memory, and I'm sure he felt he should have remembered the regulation in question. His memory was in fact phenomenal. But it had to be more than just phenomenal; it had to be the best anywhere around.

"Al Smith's got a terrific memory," I remarked one day. "I heard a bunch of reporters talking about it."

"How so?" Fiorello wanted to know. He was rising to the bait nicely, a fine querulous edge to his voice.

"It's just terrific, that's how so. Somebody mentioned a certain obscure law not long ago, and Al Smith reeled off its year, chapter, and number."

"Was he being interviewed in a law library at the time?"

"I don't know," I said, taken aback somewhat. "Probably not; why?"

"Because if he wasn't, he was safe. Al Smith's smart all right—smart enough to know reporters are too lazy to check up on a thing like that. He could have said anything that popped into his head; *they'd* never be the wiser."

Come to think of it, Fiorello was seldom charitable in his utterances concerning reporters or the press in general; and to the New York press in particular he was *never* charitable. He considered the Washington press to be of a higher caliber because, unlike the New Yorkers, he said, they would respect an "off the record" statement. In fact, when holding a press conference in Manhattan, he would often say witheringly: "This is absolutely confidential and not for publication. So don't mention my name when you print it!"

I'm not sure, but I think his sporadic forays against the fourth estate dated from its bitter assault on him when he first opposed the Sales Tax. A good many editorials had been absolutely scurrilous, even going so far as to question his patriotism. I'm sure this had hurt him more deeply than he ever let on; at any rate I know he had me clip and give him every abusive comment I could find.

He was in Washington when I read headlines one night that made my hair curl: "La Guardia Charges Press Crooked." Oh, Lord, I thought. This time he *has* done it. This time the charges are too flimsy and the defendants too many, too powerful, and too articulate. I was sick with worry for him. Like hundreds of other people I had still not learned that Fiorello could take care of himself with anything from adverbs to cutlasses. Unable to stand it any longer, I called him from my apartment at ten o'clock that night. He was dismayed that a "boy" was wasting his money on long-distance calls, and instructed me to hang up at once. I hadn't had a chance to get a word in edgewise. Finally I got the word "papers" through to him.

"What's that?"

"The papers. They're all saying you've attacked the press."

"Fine," he said. "That's swell. Now hang up."

"But they say you called them robbers, cheap confidence men, swindlers—"

"That's right. They quoted me correctly. They are, too. Now *I'm* going to hang up. You go to bed. Or better still, get some work done."

I spent a sleepless night thinking of the hammer blows that would surely rain down upon us in the morning.

But the morning editorials, incredibly, either ignored his attack or else made mollifying noises about it. All organizations made mistakes in personnel, they intoned too reasonably, and newspapers were not exempt from human fallibility; they welcomed honest criticism, found it valuable; Mr. La Guardia's statements were perhaps extreme; but they contained substance worth exploring, and served as a cogent reminder that eternal vigilance, and so on and so forth. I was stunned.

The evening papers followed suit. And all of them, I knew, would cheerfully have slit his throat. How had he done it? Like Wambsganss' unassisted triple play in the 1921 World Series: How in hell could he have done it?

I met him at the station that Friday, full of eager questions. He shrugged them off, as though the whole thing was hardly worthy of discussion—a mere border skirmish, a patrol action. Which meant he was going to let me stew in my own juice, one of his favorite recipes, until he was good and ready to tell me about it.

When he finally broke down and told me what had happened, it was in an elaborately casual manner, similar in mood to those peasant hunter pictures in which a man matter-of-factly relates the bare details of the hunt, secure in the knowledge that such an unadorned recital can only emphasize the enormous skill of the hunter.

"I just called them in," he said. "I told them their financial editors were crooked. I had two stacks of affidavits in front of me, one large stack and one small one. I picked up the small stack and said, 'Here is the sworn proof of the rigging of Indian Motorcycle and Purol stocks by editors of some of your *very* respectable New York papers. Now, I have demonstrated my point: your rags are crooked. However, should your superiors doubt it, I will in that case be glad to release this *big* stack of additional affidavits relating to a good many other stocks tomorrow. In fact, I'll even read the whole thing into the *Congressional Record* for them, as they may not want to use up so much of their own valuable space as would be required for a full account.' Well," concluded Fiorello with deep satisfaction, "I still have the big stack of affidavits—and nobody wants to see them."

Then he laughed and laughed. Finally he said, very seriously, as though it were something he wanted me to learn and remember: "Show your reserves—but never commit them."

The subject of newspapers came up again some months later, and we had quite a set-to about it. After all, I had worked for one, and my loyalty was aroused by Fiorello's taunts. He scoffed at the idea that newspapers fought Special Privilege: they got special privileges for themselves on mail rates, didn't they? The notion that newspapers cared about Justice was laughable: one squinty eye on Justice to make sure she didn't make any false moves in the paper's direction, and the other winking seductively at space buyers. I knew he was just needling me, but this time it was I who rose to the bait, unable to restrain myself:

"If you think all the ones being published now are so bad, why don't you start one up yourself and run it the way you think it should be run!"

"By God, I'd like to! Only, I'd have to publish a new one every week, there'd be so many libel suits against each one."

"Of course, you'd have to accept advertising in order to exist," I said. "You'd have to solicit it. Very humiliating for you. You might even have to compromise a lofty principle or two in order to get it."

"I would not. I'd get all the advertising I wanted simply by sitting back and waiting for it to come in. I'd pick and choose what I wanted to run, too. And furthermore, I'd get it all in New York City."

"How? By getting Congress to pass a law making it illegal to advertise with anybody but you?"

"Nope. I'd simply publish every judgment taken against installment buyers on the front page, with a warning to people to stay away from these particular concerns. Why, just think how the furniture companies would come running with ads to undo the damage and prevent any more of the same. I'd take 'em, too," he finished, "and with the money I'd start a new sheet to expose how they'd tried to knife me on the old one." He was terribly pleased with his own ingenuity.

"Well, anyway," I said, "you have to admit that newspapers are for good government and law enforcement."

He cocked a sardonic eyebrow at me. *"Everybody* is for good government and law enforcement, Ernest," he said with finality. *"But only if it applies to the other guy."*

Cynicism did not come naturally to Fiorello; it had been forced upon him by harsh experience, and he resented it. He was by nature essentially idealistic and sentimental. There were times when his sentimentality was harder to take than his caustic tongue. He had, for example, a misty-eyed concept of "Youth" that often embarrassed and infuriated all of us in the office under the age of thirty-five. "Youth" was sacred, pure, and vulnerable. It was a hell of a thing to have to live up to. When a great hullaballo was made over a shocking incident involving the killing of a Hawaiian by a Navy officer, Fiorello refused to discuss the case with me, though he himself was in consultation with the Justice Department on it. It was too sordid; "Youth" ought not to be exposed to such things, ought not even to know they existed. I used to wonder what he thought my days and nights as a Broadway reporter had been like. No matter; he insisted on making me feel like a superannuated Boy Scout, scrubbed knees, shiny shoes, cowlick and all.

I remember him talking very earnestly one day to a man older than himself about the Younger Generation. I was busy at the filing cabinets and of course made no attempt not to listen. He spoke of Today's Youth as though we were all a bunch of helpless rabbits without a brain in the crowd, wide open to the onslaughts of evil hawks. At one point he gestured broadly in my direction: I was Exhibit A. I couldn't interrupt, so I just slammed the files shut with considerable force and stalked out, steaming. Fiorello pretended not to notice. In the outer office Mimi looked up inquiringly. I grumbled that I was Pure Youth again and was pretty sick of it.

"Well," Mimi said reflectively, "it's better than being a Menace to Progress."

As befits a shielder of the young and a prophet to boot, Fiorello was the most rigid of Calvinists. He swore like a trooper, but I never heard him utter a filthy word. As for dirty jokes, he was fastidious to the point of squeamishness. Remember the headline "Smoot Smites Smut"? Fiorello would have seen no humor in it, nor would Cotton Mather's attitude toward salaciousness have seemed extreme. A sudden outburst of raucous laughter in the outer office propelled him out of his sanctum one morning. He stood there looking at us like a disapproving schoolmarm.

"What's so funny?"

No one spoke.

"Oh," he said disgustedly, and retired.

It had been a very mild joke. When I went inside an hour or so later I offered to repeat it. He was wary. "Only if it's funny," he said dubiously. I delivered it, and after a slight pause he smiled wanly. It wasn't funny, but it wasn't actually offensive either. It was just barely passable. I never told him one again.

Another pet *idée fixe* of Fiorello's bore the magic label "Progress." When Naval appropriations suffered a huge cut, and it looked as though Navy dirigibles were going to come under the ax, Fiorello was aghast. Dirigibles represented Progress. Never mind about the *Shenandoah*, that ill fated craft that had broken up in midair a few years before: accidents would happen, but Progress must be unimpeded. With the dismal prospect of the gigantic *Akron* headed for the junk heap urging him on, Fiorello got together with ranking Naval airmen, and together they began mapping out a campaign.

I was told to work up a memo on the history of lighter-than-air craft, with some conclusions. I went into the subject with great care. Subjectively, I was pulled in opposite directions: I certainly wasn't opposed to Progress, but I couldn't quite obliterate from my mind the terrible image of the *Shenandoah*'s sailors being pitched helplessly round and round in the wild sky. On the facts alone, however,

I came to the conclusion that the day of the mammoth dirigible was over, and that was the finding in the memo I handed to Fiorello.

He read it slowly, and when he was finished he put it down gently and with great deliberation took off his glasses. My heart sank. I knew this mood only too well: pained surprise, deep dejection, and an awful sort of gentle reproach. It was one of his most effective routines. He smiled a mortician's smile and shook his head sadly. "At one time, Ernest—" he said, and looked away, unable to continue.

"Yes?" I prompted resignedly.

"At one time I had high hopes for you. But no longer. No longer."

"Why, what's the matter, Major?"

He simply shook his head again.

"All right," I said. "So we disagree on the subject. But my reasons are sound. And," I added defiantly, "my opinion about big dirigibles is shared by the majority of the Congress."

"I'm not thinking now about dirigibles, Ernest. I'm thinking about *you*." He tapped my memo with his glasses. "This shows," he said sepulchrally, "that you are against Progress. That you are, in fact, a Menace to Progress. I never believed it before. But now—" He gazed at the memo as though it were unclean, something he would like to deny the existence of but couldn't.

"Look," I exploded, "dirigibles—"

"I've told you, Ernest, it's not a question of dirigibles. It's—" but again he was unable to go on; the disappointment was too crushing. He waved me away. At the door

I glanced back; he was slumped in his chair like Thiers getting the peace terms from Bismarck.

I began complaining bitterly to Mimi, but neither he nor anyone else wanted any part of my problem. It was a well known fact that Fiorello seldom doghoused one at a time. Once he got started he generally ended up with a kennelful. Nobody was anxious to be next.

Nothing happened, though, and when he bounced out of his office about five o'clock it was obvious that he had undergone a startling transformation. He was positively exuberant.

"Come along, Ernest," he cried. "Come along!"

When we were out in the corridor he patted my shoulder. "It's all right," he said reassuringly. "You're not against Progress."

"No?" I asked, pleased but bewildered.

"Nope. You just don't know what the hell you're talking about."

Something, of course, had happened to cheer him up. Later on I found out that a call had come through with the information that a compromise would be agreed upon: no more huge dirigibles, but a program of small ones instead. Like Napoleon, Fiorello could content himself with the best slice he could get if he couldn't have the whole loaf. And now he was able to administer to me a pat on the shoulder that was also a kick in the pants—a talent at which he was unsurpassed by any man.

VII

My people were of the more reserved industrial Mediterranean North, Genoa, but they could scarcely be called phlegmatic. Fiorello's were from Foggia—much more artistic and musical, and far more expansive. We seldom discussed our common heritage of race, but when the Lindbergh baby was kidnaped, Fiorello did say to me, "I hope that bastard kidnaper doesn't turn out to be Italian." So did I. The Italian immigration had taken place only three decades before, and its publicized effects on the country were mostly lamentable, centering around tabloid headlines about the Capones, Fiaschettis, Costellos, and similar scum of gangland. These lice were as typical of the Italian immigrant as John Dillinger was typical of the American Midwesterner. People knew John Dillinger wasn't representative, but they tended to think of Capone as a prototype of the Italian-American. It was particularly galling to both Fiorello and myself to hear cheap Italian politicians brag about Italy's culture in broken English to polyglot audiences, when both speakers and audiences were quite probably under the impression that Da Vinci was the featherweight champion and Donatello a second baseman for Rochester. It was embarrassing as well as galling, and there was no need for us to put our feelings into words. Each understood how the other felt.

I remember hearing it said that the northern Europeans converse in words; that the eastern Mediterraneans, the Greeks and Jews particularly, converse by means of words and gestures; and that the western Mediterraneans, particularly the Italians, converse by means of gestures alone. This theory I believe has merit. The raised eyebrow, the stroked chin, the quick grimace, the long face, the outstretched palms, the wagging nod, the imperceptible shrug —these comprised a vocabulary understood by both Fiorello and me. I spoke no Italian and seldom heard any at home, but I learned, perhaps unconsciously, my father's way of staring at or through or away from something, each look speaking volumes. So Fiorello and I often communicated without speech. And this, too, was a factor in our friendship, for friendship depends in part on effortless communication.

Fiorello liked history, and I was crazy about it. In fact, the range of our interests was wide, catholic, and in a great many instances identical. In argument I hurled my theories and hypotheses against his facts and experience, and he enjoyed the exchange—perhaps because his were the more effective weapons and he seldom lost. He trusted my sense of honor and, as so often happens in such cases, I did my best never to give him reason not to. Had he had any doubts on the matter, our relationship would have died aborning. Once having satisfied himself on that score, as I have no doubt he took pains to do, he could relax with me. Also, since I was not in the acute financial straits of most of the people in his district, an evening with me was a respite from the emotional pressures of the day.

Of course, in many ways we differed. For one thing, Fiorello was unforgiving. If he was personally wronged, he seldom forgave or forgot it. Knowing Fiorello made me understand how Rome could send ten legions to punish traitorous Syracuse, reserving only four to stand against Hannibal at the gates of Rome itself. Like a Roman, Fiorello could be reasonably philosophic, even generous, about the spear of his foe in his chest, but the knife of a foe in his back called for vengeance, and the wound never healed. Too, he was completely different from me in his scrutiny of detail in personal matters. He kept his voluminous files up to the minute, and Stromboli and Vesuvius combined were small-time compared to the La Guardian eruption if a single paper was missing. He was a prolific letter writer; I never wrote when I could telephone, and the A.T. & T. system was expanding to remote regions. I was skeptic; he was evangelistic; I thought in terms of potential; he in terms of the inevitable.

But all these generalities became evident to me only after the passage of years. At the moment I was too busy to take the long view—too busy absorbing the drama that was going on around us, too busy trying to keep myself out of hot water, too busy coping with the immediate chores and dilemmas of the daily round. Looking back, I can recall a wide variety of situations involving Fiorello and myself, but nearly all of them had in common some element of comedy, whether either of us realized it at the time or not. Even serious, essentially tragic matters sometimes managed to provide a spark of humor—not in themselves, of course, but in their conjunction with the peculiar chemical reaction that seemed to take place whenever Fiorello and I got together on any given subject.

We often discussed major issues together, but my role was mostly as devil's advocate; I think it helped Fiorello to articulate his thoughts, just to see how they sounded out loud. Consequently, I was often the audience for a dress rehearsal in New York; a few days later I would read the reviews of the opening in Washington. I remember one serious crisis, however, on which he did invite my opinion.

In the spring of 1932 a ragged trickle of veterans seeking a Veterans' Bonus started to flow toward Washington. Before long the trickle had swelled to an ominous torrent. The veterans gathered together in wretched huts on the desolate Anacostia flats at the elbow of the Potomac River. There arose from this makeshift camp a dangerous rumble not unlike the beginnings of a major avalanche. The whole country expected trouble. When Fiorello asked me what I thought about it, I said I believed it should be dealt with as a health problem. I also said that the assembly of angry veterans was a symptom of a national disease that should be treated at its source. Unless this were done, I felt it mattered very little how the current crisis was handled. In fact, I was opposed to the payment of the bonus because that would be tantamount to conferring special privileges on only one segment of a more inclusive problem.

At first Fiorello said nothing. It was an election year, and I wondered if he was considering the poor economic condition of his own district. If he took the same view that I did on the bonus issue, it might very well do him considerable damage locally. On problems of major importance, however, Fiorello was quite capable of taking a position running counter to his own immediate interests; in fact, when the time came he voted against the bonus. I don't flatter myself that his ultimate stand was influenced in any way by my opinion. Our points of view simply happened to coincide.

Though Fiorello jeopardized the veteran's vote in his own district by coming out against the bonus, he labored unceasingly to alleviate the plight of the veterans congregated in Washington. He urged barracks and food and clothing for them. He originated the idea that their fare home be paid on request. On the ugly day that the Bonus Army was ejected by force, Fiorello was beside himself with rage. We followed the dire reports as they came over the wires. At the outset no one knew how extensive the casualties were and, of course, the wildest of unfounded rumors were abroad: women had been shot, and babies gassed.

Fiorello came stamping out of his office with the draft of a telegram to the White House. "What do you think of *that?*" he said, slamming it on my desk. It read: "Beans is better than bullets and soup is better than gas—F. La Guardia."

For reasons I cannot fathom to this very day I replied in all seriousness, "You've got to say 'Beans *are* better than bullets' or: 'A bean *is* better than *a* bullet.'" His expression unnerved me, but I rambled on more and more lamely: "You see, you can't have a plural subject with a verb in the singular—"

Sometimes I think my right ear is still ringing. "A wise

guy!" he shrieked. "The Capitol in flames and *you* talk *grammar*. Wise guy!"

He flung back into his office, and I just sat there, blinking. The door flew open again almost immediately and he reappeared, still mad as a hornet. He pointed scornfully at me and shouted to the girl who had typed up the wire: "Change it! Give him his way! Give the college boy his way!" Then he stamped his foot and cried, "Shame!" and vanished once more into his office.

The telegram went off and so did I, home to sulk for a couple of days. I was beginning to think that Achilles must have got mighty sick and tired of his tent when one of the girls called to say that the Major wanted to know what was wrong with me. I had half expected this call and had prepared an eloquent tirade in my own defense. I was, therefore, somewhat astonished to hear myself saying weakly that I had been busy but would be around the next morning. Actually, I returned to the office within the hour. I couldn't wait to get back.

Not long after this episode Fiorello was asked to sponsor an amateur boxing show at the Star Casino, the proceeds to go to an organization connected with relief for the unemployed. He was handling the assignment along more or less routine lines until one of the people arranging the actual bouts told him about a terrific young Irish heavyweight who had agreed to fight in the main event provided a suitable opponent could be found. Fiorello said he knew just the man; he wouldn't reveal his name now but this was a boy who would knock the Irishman cold within the first three rounds. And who do you suppose this peerless pugilist turned out to be? Me.

When I discovered what Fiorello had in mind, I was so taken aback that I could hardly speak. He began by telling me what a marvelous opportunity it was for me, and I could see that he was gradually working himself up to a point where he would be convinced that he had had to work hard to secure for me this chance of a lifetime. I knew that his enthusiasm had to be nipped in the bud. I interrupted him in mid-sentence with the firm statement that nothing this side of heaven or hell would get me into a fight ring. For one thing, I said, I had been a pro football player, and the Irishman would lose his amateur standing by fighting a mixed bout. Fiorello waved this away: Murray Hulbert, the kingpin of amateur athletics, was a good friend of his and there would be no problem about our getting a special dispensation. It was regrettable, of course, that I had demeaned myself by accepting money for my athletic prowess, but he felt sure that he could get the rules relaxed on my behalf in this instance, since the whole thing was, after all, for sweet charity's sake.

I then protested that it would be no contest whatsoever. I said I had done a little rough-and-tumble boxing and wrestling, but that under the Marquis of Queensberry Rules I'd be slaughtered. I insisted that I was training to be a lawyer, not a prizefighter, and that I would not, repeat not, fight in his shindig under any circumstances. He told me coolly that he wanted me to think it over.

The next few days were a great strain. Fiorello became more and more hipped on the subject and really nagged me about it. "Ernest," he cajoled, "can't you just see that headline?" As a matter of fact I could see two alternate headlines: "Cuneo Knocked Out" if I lost, and "La Guard-

ia's Clerk Victorious" if I won. I could find no personal
nourishment in the situation at all.

Finally he came to me and said he couldn't stall any
longer; he had to name a man. I told him to go right ahead
and name somebody, anybody but me. He said that if I
didn't have the sense to grab this chance he would be
forced to call on the Marines. I told him I thought that that
was a perfectly bully idea. He said he didn't want to hear
me going around afterward saying I hadn't had a crack at
the chance. I promised him I wouldn't say that. He just
wanted to tell me that there were to be no recriminations
from me after it was too late. I assured him there would be
no recriminations and for God's sake to call in the Marines.
At long last he got the idea that I wasn't really enthusiastic
and he went away, shaking his head. The Marines accepted.

We went to the fights together and had ringside seats.
Finally the main event rolled around. The Irishman was
the first on the scene, charging into the ring like an An-
dalusian bull into a Madrid arena. He had the long wiry
legs of a lad who could go the distance. His superstructure
was equally impressive: long arms, the sloping shoulders
of a born puncher, and heavy deltoid and pectoral muscles
that bespoke long hours at the weight machine. His long
tawny hair fell over his forehead as he jigged himself loose.
He bobbed and weaved in the Dempsey crouch. He
looked confident and speedy: about twenty-four, six feet
one in his stockings, and 190 stripped. I shifted happily in
my seat, very glad to be exactly where I was.

The house darkened and the Marines came down the
aisle, two seconds in dress blues and the heavyweight in a

striking bathrobe in the colors of the Corps. There was a fanfare of trumpets as they entered the ring. Fiorello leaned over and whispered bitterly, "That could have been you." I nodded and tried to look rueful. Then we all stood up and sang "The Star-Spangled Banner," and I can't remember ever singing it with more spirit.

The Marine's bathrobe slipped from his shoulders. He was big and young, not more than nineteen or twenty, and weighed in at about 210. His hair was very black and his skin very pink and white. He was well muscled, but his legs were heavy for a boxer. Altogether he looked a little downy and a bit soft. When he came to the center of the ring to receive the referee's instructions, he seemed nervous.

The bell clanged. The Irishman flew across the ring like a hawk descending on a wood pigeon. There was a brief flurry that ended with a left hook to the Marine's solar plexus and a wicked right that crossed home to the point of his chin. The Marine was on the canvas. He was so green he started to get up before taking the benefit of the count. The Irishman hovered over him and was motioned to a neutral corner by the referee. He circled to the one behind the Marine—ringwise and a killer. Meanwhile, the Marine looked exactly like the Dying Gaul. At the count of seven he swayed to his feet. The Irishman angled in sharply and the maneuver was repeated, except that this time the Marine's head hit the canvas immediately in front of Fiorello and me. It was all over in the first minute and a half. His buddies carried him to his corner and quickly brought him to. He stood up a minute later and gave the crowd a shy, almost apologetic smile. He was given a big hand as he clambered out of the ring and trudged up the aisle to the dressing rooms.

Fiorello refused to meet my eye. "Don't say it," he snapped.

We stopped by for a chat with the Marine before we left. He was a nice boy. He said he was sorry he hadn't made a better showing against the Irishman. Fiorello told him to forget it, he'd done fine. "At least," said Fiorello pointedly, "the spirit was willing, and that's what counts."

On the way home I pointed out that I was an ideal chopping block—5'9½" and 188 pounds—for a taller and heavier man in the same division. "Sure," Fiorello said sarcastically, "the short guys never get anywhere. Look at Frank Moran, Jack Dillon, and Mickey Walker." I admitted that these men were exceptions that had proved the rule, but I pointed out with some asperity that none of them had won their laurels while putting in ten hours a day as law clerks. We bade each other a chilly good night.

I'm afraid there were times when I deliberately did my best to get under Fiorello's skin just to see how loudly he'd howl. I particularly remember one balmy summer evening when Fiorello suggested that we take in the Lewisohn Stadium concert. He said he felt like having some boiled beef for dinner first. Not only was this a favorite dish of his, but he was a minor authority on its preparation. I said I knew a continental restaurant near the Columbia campus that always carried boiled beef on its menu. He asked me if I had ever tried it and I said No, but that I had always liked what I'd had there. He seemed dubious but we went.

He had a long, involved conversation with the maître d'
full of esoteric German expressions. They seemed very
pleased with themselves and each other before it was over.
I remember this because it was the only time I ever saw
Fiorello at all particular about his food. When it came it
seemed to me no better and no worse than boiled beef
usually tastes, but Fiorello pronounced it delicious. Toward the end of the meal he fell into a reverie and, as
though from a great distance, said, "Heaven is Budapest at
dawn in May." I asked him what he meant by that, but he
shrugged it off. It probably had some connection with
boiled beef.

We rode out to the stadium by bus. It was a beautiful
evening and I felt good. Like arguing. I asked him if he
didn't agree that Art was a Universal. He did. I said that
therefore pure art in one form could be translated into
pure art in some other form, otherwise it could not have
been Pure Art in the first place. For instance, I said, archi-
tecture had been described as frozen music. I asked him if
he ever thought of Riverside Church as frozen music. He
said No, he never had and what's more he never intended
to. He also said that Raymond Fosdick, the rector's brother,
had asked for compensation of some sort for the YMCA
at the end of the war and that he had countered with a bill
to charge the YMCA rent. He added that people who
talked about Pure Art were nothing but word acrobats and
maybe bores, too. This was just the prickly frame of mind I
wanted him in.

Many people spoke to him as we made our way to our
seats. A good many pleasant, cultivated people stopped by

to pay their respects. I noticed that the conversations were all about music. They recognized in Fiorello a fellow devotee as knowledgeable and appreciative as they. When the music began Fiorello gave it his rapt attention and he applauded vigorously at the conclusion of the first number. Then came a ballet, and I heard him give a slight groan as a trio of muscular male dancers pranced on.

"What's the matter?" I asked.

"They make me sick," said Fiorello.

"Well!" I said. "I thought you loved the Arts. Now I find you don't."

"I just don't like those guys," he muttered.

"Well!" I said again, doing my best to look profoundly shocked.

On the way out after the concert was over, I went on being mystified, shaking my head and biting my lip, hoping he would ask what was wrong with me, which he presently did. I said I couldn't understand why he hated ballet. I said his attitude was disillusioning to me. We were climbing the hill to our bus, and I could see that at last I was getting his goat.

"Listen," he said. "You know what I'd do if I had charge of the arts? I'd let those guys dance *once* for Art's sake and then shoot them."

I frowned solemnly. "But that would be a terrible thing to do," I said. "Before long there wouldn't be any ballet. Now I'm sure you don't love Art."

"All right," he said, "I'd let 'em dance *twice*."

"It seems to me," I said after a moment of deep thought, "that if you were going to shoot them you shouldn't have let them dance in the first place. Maybe they could have found expression elsewhere, because Art is Universal, remember. We're agreed about that."

We were at the top of the hill. "*We're* agreed?" he said in exasperation.

"Sure," I said, "We *agreed* on that."

"Listen," he said firmly. "An apple and a piece of horse manure were floating down the Mississippi. All the way down from St. Paul they bobbed along together. When they got down to the last bend above New Orleans, the piece of horse manure said to the apple, 'Well, I see we're getting into New Orleans,' and the apple said, 'Listen, brother, from now on just knock off that *we* business.'" He peered at me over his glasses and, to make sure I hadn't missed the point, he said, "I'm the apple," and laughed uproariously.

We got on the bus and started off. Opposite Grant's Tomb I suddenly said to him, "After what you've said tonight I'm surprised you're not a member of the Socialist Party." This sent Fiorello into a long dissertation, the main point of which was that Socialists were too dogmatic. I never heard a more dogmatic attack on dogmatism. I mentioned Norman Thomas. He said that Norman Thomas was dogmatic, too. "For that matter," he said, "the Republicans are too dogmatic. They found out I wouldn't take their guff when I supported La Follette in 1924. It's a good thing for us, Ernest, that the Republicans know nothing of party discipline, otherwise we'd be in the soup."

"*We?*" I asked pointedly.

"Sure," he said grandly. "*We*." He was the coach handing me back my jersey after having benched me. I was back on the team again.

Being on the team was sometimes a little like being thrust upon a stage without lines or an adequate costume. None of us in the office could ever be sure what sort of character we might be assigned next by Fiorello, the casting director. Usually, however, it was one of two extremes, either the heavy in *The Black Crook* or Little Eva in *Uncle Tom's Cabin*. One was either handed a halo and lauded as Thomas Jefferson's only spiritual heir, or a pitchfork and denounced as the unnatural descendant of Benedict Arnold. One thing was certain: whatever role one drew, Fiorello played *his* with the greatest of relish and éclat. This theatrical metaphor is entirely apropos. Fiorello was a theatrical sort of person, a great actor in the best and warmest sense of the word: he was always able to convey perfectly the emotion he was feeling at any given moment and, conversely, could sincerely feel the emotion he wanted to convey. He was, in addition, an inspired mimic with an enviable gift for satiric caricature. Also, he instinctively knew how to extract every ounce of drama from any situation whatsoever and how to sustain it. This necessitated, of course, the involvement, voluntary or otherwise, of innocent bystanders who served in a passive way to complete the scene Fiorello chose to play. Whether they liked it or not they were as powerless to resist the compelling tide of dramaturgy as a box of shredded wheat being borne to the lip of Niagara Falls. For example, there were two dramatically charged episodes into both of which I was dragooned as a sort of glorified walk-on.

Fiorello had the idea of levying heavy state and federal

taxes on the New York Stock Exchange. He was ready to flay the skin from their hides. One of the governors of the Stock Exchange caused it to be known that they could always carry on from Jersey City to escape New York State taxation, or from Canada, if necessary, to escape federal taxation. Whoever cooked up this fatuous idea left Fiorello much in his debt, because that was exactly the tack he wanted them to take. "Rats deserting a sinking ship" was his description of their attitude. He accused them of plotting a panic, which wasn't funny, because that was a crime, and there was, in fact, a quiet one already on.

He sent me a telegram from Washington stating that all had failed him; even the Library of Congress couldn't find it; nobody knew where it was, but Woodrow Wilson had once said that if the financiers continued their fight against him he promised them a "gallows higher than Haman's." Get that quotation. Everything depends on it —everything. And get it by tomorrow, too. It was no less than Roland's call. I could see he was terribly exercised when he wrote it.

Nobody in the office knew who the hell Haman was or why he was hanged, and neither did I. Mimi agreed to find out for me, because I was obviously going to have my work cut out for me, locating the quote in the huge mass of Wilsoniana. My mind racing along on all cylinders, I swiftly concluded that if the Library of Congress couldn't find Wilson's speech, then neither could I. But it was late afternoon and I had to do something—fast. I fell back on my reporter's training and found in the Washington Telephone Directory the number of a Joseph Tumulty. Tumulty had been Mr. Wilson's secretary. I put in a person-to-person call and prayed. It was the right Joseph Tumulty, hurrah, but he was out golfing at the Congressional Country Club, *damn*. The call was put through there. Mr. Tumulty was out on the links, but should be in shortly. I waited, gnawing at my nails. When the phone rang I tremblingly picked up the receiver. Having decided to go it alone, I didn't mention the office. I said: "Mr. Tumulty, my name is Ernest Cuneo. I'm a law student. A little question came up, a minor point of information you may have."

"Well, what is it?" a pleasant voice asked.

"Mr. Wilson," I said, "once remarked that if the financiers fought him, he would give them a gallows higher than Haman's. Do you know where and when he said that?"

"No," said Mr. Tumulty, "I do not recall. But I'll tell you a funny coincidence: Congressman La Guardia called me yesterday and asked me that very same question." Ouch! I was glad I hadn't identified myself.

"He did?" I said weakly.

"Yes, he did," said Mr. Tumulty, with a hint of suspicion in his voice now. I thanked him hurriedly and rang off.

I was now desperate. Who else? An idea struck me: Ray Stannard Baker, Wilson's biographer. I got in touch with his publishers and they gave me his number up in New Hampshire after hearing a précis of my plight. I called him. Eureka! He knew all about it. I felt giddy with success. Baker said I'd find it in volume so-and-so, page such-and-such. Wilson's speech had been delivered in Chicago, after he was elected but before he took office for the first time. I bounded to the library like a happy gazelle and, of course, there it was, cold.

Having learned from Fiorello himself how to exploit every ounce of drama from any given situation, I phrased my answering telegram as if it had been composed between yawns. His query, I reported, had called to mind something I remembered reading in Wilson's biography, and a quick check had proved it to be so. He would find the quotation in Ray Stannard Baker's work on Wilson, citation as follows, and so on. Off went the telegram. Mimi came in shortly thereafter with the intelligence that Haman was a biblical character, a complete louse who was hanged on a gallows he had prepared for someone else.

That night I got the longest and most effusive telegram I ever hope to receive. I had Saved the Day. The Library of Congress was quivering with shame. Youth had brought Blithering Old Age to its knees, if not to its senses. The White House staff researchers were no better. They too had failed. "But you, Ernest—" It ran on like that for pages. I said nothing about the telegram at the office the next morning beyond the bare statement that I had heard from the Major and that he seemed pleased.

The next time Fiorello put in an appearance he was a Man with a Message. He called us all in to his sanctum. He was standing in back of his chair, and as we trooped in he motioned me around to his right side. The others stood facing us. He began talking to them. "Look at this boy," he said. They all did. I shifted my weight to my other foot. "Look at him—and from now on, treat him with great respect!" He paused for effect, and everyone looked more puzzled than before. Mimi looked like a bored and weary super on an opera stage for whom there are no surprises left but who will lug his spear anywhere they tell him. "*Because*," said Fiorello, with emphatic conviction, "he's going to be the first Latin President of the United States!" My fellow workers did their best to look impressed, but without much success. We just exchanged embarrassed glances. "You'll be proud that you knew him," Fiorello went on; but now his eye fell on his mail and he sat down abruptly and started to read it, forgetting all about us.

Out we filed, closing the door quietly behind us. It was exactly thirteen seconds by the sweep hand of my watch before I was addressed as "Mr. President" by Mimi in mock-deferential tones. It developed into an office joke, because we all knew that the fruit fly had a prolonged existence compared to my probable tenure of office as Fiorello's President.

My impeachment came even sooner than I had expected. A couple of days later Fiorello said that while I had many fine qualities I lacked discipline. I admitted that this was true. Then he said that I had no concept of what a struggle it was to maintain law and order. I said I doubted that. He had thought it over carefully, he said, and had decided that what I needed was a couple of months under his good friend J. Edgar Hoover. He went on about what a wonderful Public Servant J. Edgar Hoover was, with a capital *P* and a capital *S*. He enlarged upon the great privilege it would be to work for him, and in fact grew so lyrical about it all that I became doubly suspicious. He spoke as though I were a high-school pitcher getting a chance to go in for one inning in the World Series. I gingerly expressed enthusiasm, not so sure I wasn't being sent back to the West Texas League.

"When would I start?" I asked warily.

"Listen," he said decisively. "You start—*maybe*—if you pass the F.B.I. examination and Hoover accepts you. That's when you start."

My emotions were mixed. I had the mortified feeling of having shown up at the White House gates for a Presidential Dinner and of my invitation being found not in order; but fortified, however, with the inner knowledge that I hadn't been anxious to go in the first place. "Gee, I didn't know it was that exclusive," I said with poorly simulated animation.

"Well, it is," said Fiorello, "and all I'm hoping is that you don't disgrace me."

"What does Mr. Hoover think about the idea?" I asked.

Fiorello looked at me as if I were mad to think he would mention a trivial nobody like me to so eminent a personage as Hoover. "He doesn't think anything about it," he said, "because I never spoke to him about it."

The next day Fiorello told me to go to a midtown address the following morning: the F.B.I. examinations were on and they would take the best part of the day, so (magnanimously) I didn't have to come into the office. I was annoyed; I thought I should have had more notice so that I could have prepared, and I said so. He said he was sure I would have no difficulty with the exams and not to worry. But I did.

The F.B.I. takes only graduate accountants or lawyers as agents, and in this depression era I knew competition would be keen. There were a lot of men taking the exams, which resembled a Bar examination in its questions, with emphasis on Evidence and Criminal Law. It wasn't too hard, but there was a minor question based on *habeas corpus ad testificandum,* and I just didn't know what the writ was.

Fiorello called me into his office first thing next morning and asked me how I thought I had done. I told him the various questions and the answers I had given; and he was nodding, going along with me so to speak, until I got to the one I said had stumped me on *habeas corpus ad testificandum.* He jerked bolt upright in his chair as if he had been prodded with some prankster's electrical shocker.

"You *don't* know what a *habeas corpus ad testificandum* is?" he said with the blank incredulity of a man who had just watched the full moon explode.

"No," I said, "I don't."

He repeated the question, and I sheepishly repeated my negative. It didn't seem awfully important to me, but Fiorello acted as if I were not only the little boy who had failed in his plain duty by not putting his finger in the dyke, but who had, in fact, attacked it with a pick.

He buzzed insistently for the whole office to come in. In they came. Once again I was standing alone, over on Fiorello's right.

His jaw was very set. I felt precisely like a prisoner in dock—an unauthorized young ensign being court-martialed for having accidentally struck the Flag of the U.S.S. *Constitution* at the very moment of victory.

"Can you imagine this?" he began. "Ernest took the F.B.I. examination yesterday and was unable to describe a *habeas corpus ad testificandum.* Can you *imagine* it?" He looked at them with an expression of mutual understanding, as if they too could surely understand the enormity of the offense.

They tried to respond but no one actually spoke. "Yes," said Fiorello, pursuing them, "that's what happened. What do you think of *that?*" His eyes were for the men; the girls were out of it, and they showed palpable relief. Mimi looked blank, Nick shot me a helpless glance, and little Gene was staring at Fiorello, transfixed. Nick moved his head from side to side, trying to look like a man who has received grave news. Mimi pursed his lips in a vain attempt to make his expressionless face look concerned.

This wasn't enough for Fiorello. He decided to poll the jury. "Mimi," he said, "What do you think of it?" clearly implying that there could be but one answer.

"I guess," said Mimi carefully, "he should have known it." Fiorello nodded vigorous approval, and nodded everyone else into strong agreement with Mimi. I stood convicted by my peers. "I'll say he should have known it," Fiorello said triumphantly, and paused. They were all still nodding, like mechanical toys.

Fiorello sprung his trap:

"All right," he said, "Mimi—*tell him.* Go on and tell him."

Mimi didn't say a word. He just gave an embarrassed half-smile and looked at the floor.

"*What!*" yelped Fiorello, "you don't know, either?" He drew back, a man who had seen cataclysm piled on disaster. Horror was in his face. "Nick," he bleated, now a man pleading for a life preserver. No help. "Gene!" as if Gene were the last straw. He was. There was a long pause.

At length Fiorello raised his lowered head. Change of

pace. "People work," he rapped out, "to make a better world for Youth, and what happens?" He let the rhetorical question hang in the air. "Long years," he said sadly and deliberately, "long years of toil. And what do you get out of it?" He scanned our faces. "Disappointment. Bitter disappointment," he explained. "That's all. But you just go on." He contrived a gesture that was both an expression of woe and an order to get out. Out we filed, in silence.

An hour later we got called back in again. "All right," he said, "What's a *habeas corpus ad testificandum?*" No answer.

Just as he thought. You could show some people the way, but out of pure stubbornness they wouldn't take it. Out.

We bunched glumly in the outer office. I volunteered to go over to the Law Library during lunch hour. I did. A *habeas corpus ad testificandum,* I discovered, is merely "a writ served on a warden for the production of a prisoner whose testimony is needed at a trial." That simple. One of the girls typed out separate copies and each of us stuffed one in his pocket against the onset.

Four o'clock. Back in. We shuffled into the familiar half-circle before his desk. He was reading. After what seemed a very long time he looked up. "A *habeas corpus ad testificandum,*" he began—and we all started to talk at once. He frowned horribly and held up his hand for silence. We subsided. "A *habeas corpus ad testificandum,*" he repeated, "is a writ served on a warden for the production of a prisoner whose testimony is needed at a trial." He looked authoritative and grand, as if he were Moses reading aloud from the tablets of stone.

"We know," we chorused.

"Sure, you know—*now*," he barked. "I just told you. Out." He seemed almost cheerful.

He walked through us at quitting time with his chin up, a saddened but not a bitter man, heroically determined to carry on alone in spite of those who failed him.

I never heard from the F.B.I., and he never referred to it again.

VIII

Foreign nations, dealing with the United States, are greatly puzzled by our *de facto* Constitution. They complain that our system is such that while the Representatives and Senators at Washington represent their districts and states, no one really represents the country as a whole. And this, they say, makes for confusion and cross-purposes. For example, the Government of Canada for over twenty years was in full accord with the President and the State Department of the United States on a St. Lawrence Waterway, but the Senators of the Middle Atlantic and New England states blocked the project on the ground that it was against their sectional interests.

This indictment would not hold true of Fiorello. While it is true that the people of his Twentieth District were very poor, practically all of the legislation Fiorello offered while a Representative was on a national basis. Certainly no coal miners or farmers lived in his district, but he fought for them as hard as if they did.

To that extent, Fiorello had a Jeffersonian faith in the People's judgment. He rendered an annual report on his votes and the reasons therefor as meticulously as if it were a Price Waterhouse audit of a bank. He never talked down; he assumed that his constituents were informed, intelligent, very much interested, and entitled to know what their Congressman was doing and why. The Twentieth was in many respects like Bob La Follette's Wisconsin: soda jerks could and would argue the merits of John Stuart Mill and Jeremy Bentham. There was much wider interest in government processes than in most places.

So Fiorello always went to the People with his record—and that really was his strength. Ironically, the Roosevelt sweep of 1932 swept Fiorello out of Congress; but long before the New Deal Fiorello had offered most of its legislation in bills before Congress. Actually, as a lame duck, Fiorello, again ironically, did a great deal to launch the New Deal for F.D.R. in his few remaining months in Washington.

Considering the place the New Deal has in American history—whether one likes it or not—Fiorello's anticipation of its major reforms, long before they were effectuated, makes a strong case for plagiarism. In the two and a half years I was with him, while F.D.R. was still Governor of New York, Fiorello offered legislation permitting the R.F.C. to act as a bank of issue to new enterprises; low-cost housing he had been plugging for years; he had long been urging a five-day, forty-hour week; he had demanded unemployment insurance; he wanted bank deposits guaranteed; he had stumped for a Government bank to discount mortgages direct from farmers and small-home owners, the interest not to exceed 3 per cent; he had introduced securities and Stock Exchange regulation bills; he had sponsored bills calling for public works and public power projects; he had fought Prohibition. Almost every bit of the major legislation enacted by F.D.R. and now on the statute books had already been offered by Fiorello before Roosevelt got to Washington.

But of course he did not neglect the particular needs of his constituents. Every letter was patiently answered. His office was so regulated that the ordinary grist was handled by trained competent personnel. The veterans, the job seekers, the immigration appeals, all got as much service as an ethical Congressman's office can give. Hundreds of requests were received and referred to the proper bureaus for action. Much of the work consisted merely in furnishing the applicant with information as to proper procedure. But at no time did I ever know Fiorello to ask a Governmental favor for anyone.

I once asked Fiorello if he had taken any active part in the Sacco-Vanzetti case, guessing that the principles involved in that famous *cause célèbre* must have stirred him deeply at the time. He said he had gone to the prison and spoken to both men, but had been unable to get any direct answers to his questions. He described Sacco gripping the bars of his cell and staring past him, repeating over and over, "The world will be cleansed by my blood." It was obviously an unpleasant subject for Fiorello, and I never brought it up again.

He knew the daily life of his district. He never lost the common touch. In fact, he was the master of it. I saw him talking to an elderly Catholic priest one day, and I was forcibly struck by their common demeanor. They reminded me of two expert doctors, both terribly experienced in epidemics, in professional consultation. Only in this case the plague was poverty.

1932 groaned in, the country aching in body and sick at heart, the breadlines multiplying like the deadly spirochete in the nation's bloodstream. Many, many people came to Fiorello's office for help, and Fiorello worked like a Trojan. But on the surface he was emotionless and direct in his works of mercy. I remember how one dark, cold winter night, around six o'clock, a big man in blue overalls came in. His face was very red, really raw. His sole protection from the weather was a thick sweater under the overall suspenders. He looked like a big Provence Frenchman: heavy set, broad, bull-necked. His hair was short and bristly, like steel wool, a pepper-and-salt black-and-white close to his scalp. He said he had walked down from Harlem and he had to see Mr. La Guardia, urgently.

He stood dumbly before Fiorello's desk looking like a Cretan bull in an ancient frieze. Fiorello asked him what his problem was. The man said that his kids were cold, they were freezing, they had no gas; it had been turned off. Fiorello asked him how much he needed, and the big man said he needed a quarter. It wouldn't have been nearly so bad if he had needed fifty or a hundred dollars, some impossible sum, but a quarter! There was something outrageous about it—that this big awkward, dignified man should be so humiliated by circumstances. I can't figure out Fiorello's reaction to this day. At the mention of the cold kids, his hand was already on its way to his wallet, but simultaneously and inexplicably he started to give the man hell. He said almost angrily that even if the kids were warm they would still be hungry and that men in overalls shouldn't have hungry children.

It was a strange performance. But I think Fiorello had been torn inside by the man's story, and had got mad so that he would not cry. He handed the man some bills and told him to get home fast.

As the man turned to go, Fiorello suddenly asked if the gas company had given him any notice. The man said no, none; they had just turned the gas off. Fiorello took down his name, address, and apartment number, and curtly motioned him out.

As soon as he was gone Fiorello called the Governor's Mansion in Albany, disregarding the lateness of the hour. He insisted on getting the home number of the public Service Commissioner. Finally he got through to him. What he then called the Public Service Commission and the Public Utilities sounded like the curse of Beelzebub himself. I remember reading that somewhere in India, when two people fight they hire professional oath makers, who place themselves squarely opposite each other, while each tries to outdo the other in the demanding art of imprecation. The writer said that he had once witnessed such an encounter, and that the incredible feats of imaginative swearing he heard, coupled with the virility of the vituperation, left him "trembling with admiration." Neither of those contestants would have been in the same league with Fiorello that night. He threatened dozens of investigations, and practically dissolved the Gas Company and their "dirty, filthy hirelings," the Public Service Commission. It went on for minutes, and miles of insulation must have peeled off the telephone wires. His blast resulted in an emergency crew being ordered to turn on the man's gas immediately. Within the hour the man called back to say so. He apparently went on, in his heavy, inarticulate way, to express his gratitude to Mr. La Guardia. Fiorello listened impatiently for a moment, then snapped: "Now make sure those kids get fed. If you don't . . . come and see me again." And slammed down the receiver.

Not all the scenes in Fiorello's office were tragic. Sometimes they seemed ridiculous examples of civic schizophrenia. A young man came in one day who bore a startling resemblance to Mortimer Snerd. The resemblance was not only physical. He plunked himself down on the hard settee about 2:30, refused to state his business or his name, and firmly stated that he would speak to no one but Congressman La Guardia. The girls gently prodded him as the afternoon wore on, but he was adamant; nobody but Fiorello would do. So he just sat there. Fiorello peeped out and didn't know him and remained holed up. But there was no wearing the visitor out. He stayed and stayed, even when the office started to shut up.

Fiorello had asked me to go with him that night, and we put on our hats and coats in his room. As we went out the door and down the corridor, the young man dropped into step alongside us. "Mr. La Guardia," said the young man solemnly as we walked, "a dog bit me."

"He did?" said Fiorello incredulously, as if unable to comprehend the horror of the occurrence. "Did you get his name?"

"No," said the young man, "I didn't."

"Well," said Fiorello, "how can I do anything for you if you don't know the dog's name?"

"I guess you're right," the young man said soberly. "I should have gotten his name."

La Guardia nodded vigorously and the young man sloped off, deep in thought.

On another day a gray-haired old Italian, a very handsome man whose strong wrinkled face gave the impression of oak leaves inlaid in his cheeks, was ushered in to see the Major. He looked every inch the proud, honest peasant. His attitude was man-to-man and man of the world as he opened the conversation. Fishing into his pocket, he drew out a Magistrate's Court summons and handed it to Fiorello. As Fiorello was looking at it, the old man exclaimed, "My eighteen-year-old daughter got it against me!"

"For what?" asked Fiorello.

"For beating her," said the old man, as if that were the most natural thing in the world.

"Three times I told her not to go to the movies with this boy, but she went anyhow. When she came home at *eleven o'clock*"—he looked at Fiorello significantly—"at *eleven o'clock*, what else could I do but hit her? Now," he said, as if he had said all that was necessary to satisfy any reasonable man, "please to call up the Judge and tell him I am her father."

Fiorello measured him with his eyes; here, personified, was the gulf between the Old World and the New. "That won't do any good," he said, shaking his head slowly. "You will have to go to court."

The old man acted as if Fiorello hadn't understood. He

started to tell the whole story over again, but Fiorello stopped him. "I know," Fiorello said gently, "you are her father. But you are not allowed to strike your child in this country. She has a right to bring you to court."

The old man looked as if he himself had just been struck. Then he slumped down onto a chair, a man no longer the head of his house. He suddenly looked very old and desperately tired. Almost tenderly, Fiorello tried to explain to him that it was different here, but the old man seemed not to hear. Presently he arose and took his hat into his rough hands. Without a word he shuffled to the door and stood for a moment, his hand on the knob, his eyes unseeing. Fiorello went to him and made a gesture as if to touch him on the arm, but did not. "Funny country, isn't it, Pop?" he said softly.

The old man wheeled around with blazing eyes and lifted a clenched fist. Once again his back was straight and his head was imperiously high. "I wish—" He choked. "I wish I had missed the boat!" But the moment of last fierce resistance was over, and his shoulders sagged again under the weight of his collapsed world.

The door closed behind him.

Fiorello turned to me and said tartly: "Our old people are good people. You youngsters just don't know. That's not funny at all."

I hadn't thought it was funny, but that wasn't the point. Fiorello needed a mask behind which to conceal his feelings. If the mask had to be a makeshift annoyance with me, that was all right too.

IX

Flamboyance in the face of physical hardship or danger has never been a handicap to an aspiring political leader. Unfortunately, it is not a talent that can be handily cultivated, such as, for example, the ability to retain the full names of several thousand people. Fiorello was among the lucky minority to whom a flair for physical derring-do came naturally. In this he resembled one of his own few heroes, Theodore Roosevelt. T.R.'s dashing charge up San Juan Hill at the head of his Rough Riders (closely followed, you will recall, by a man he termed the bravest he ever knew) had appealed mightily to Fiorello's young imagination. And later, when T.R. was off terrorizing big game in remote regions of the world, Fiorello followed his exploits as breathlessly as the rest of the populace. When in later years New York's Mayor La Guardia was observed rushing off to the scene of some particularly promising conflagration, it may be that he was emulating the example of his boyhood idol. Emulating and, incidentally, profiting from that pattern, since the stuff of valor is not without its publicity value. An Elihu Root with a closely reasoned treatise in his brief case doesn't cut nearly the figure of a Roosevelt dispatching a charging lion with one bullet or a La Guardia disappearing into the smoke and flame of a blazing building.

The young Winston Churchill was possessed of the same high physical courage, picking off three men from horseback with his pistol at Omdurman and later thrilling his countrymen with his soaring words about the winging lead of the Boers. And later, when he became Home Secretary, he accompanied the Bobbies on one of their few gun battles with a desperate killer.

Fiorello's heroics were no less real or laudable. His reaction to danger of any kind was simply to plunge headlong toward it, assuming, if possible, the major risk himself. When a maniac started shooting down at the House from the visitor's gallery one time, most of the Representatives with sufficient presence of mind to move at all prudently ducked for cover, realizing themselves to be as helpless as fish in a barrel. Fiorello, however, stood up, spotted the fire area, and tore madly up the stairs to disarm the man. Fortunately, the situation was in hand before he got there. As mayor, he once boarded a burning ship loaded with high explosives and stayed aboard until the fire laddies had things under control. He had the best of times—and headlines—as the Boy on the Burning Deck. On another occasion Fiorello personally tested the validity of a responsible engineering opinion to the effect that poor ventilation had made the Park Avenue vehicular tunnel a lethal chamber of carbon monoxide by driving into the middle of it and parking there for a spell, breathing deeply the while. When he emerged he gave the air inside a clean bill of

Visit to Canada

MAN OF
MANY MOODS . . .

That'll hold 'em!

You guys sure complicate things

Ask no quarter, give no quarter

Nuts, Ernest, nuts!

You don't mean it,
my boy

Naturally, I didn't
fall for *that!*

Can't you see how simple it is?

Your move, brother

The Crusader

Hopalong

Most valuable player

health. At another time he insisted on being taken down in the sister ship of the ill fated submarine *S4*, whose sinking had generated a great public hue and cry. Whatever he observed on the run must have been indisputable evidence, because when he surfaced he told the American people that the Navy was completely exonerated.

Fiorello's lifetime devotion to aviation is easily understood: it represented the latest phase of the American pioneering spirit; it stood for Progress; it was dangerous and demanded a high degree of physical courage. His first contact with it dated from the days when he was counsel for an airplane company financed by small investors and headed by the aeronautical engineering genius Giuseppe Bellanca, the brother of labor leader August Bellanca, Sidney Hillman's strongest supporter. Within a couple of years he had learned to fly. When World War I came along, this fact, taken together with his linguistic abilities, resulted in his appointment as Commanding Officer of the U.S. Air Branch on the Italian-Austrian front.

I heard quite a lot from Fiorello about his war experiences, but almost everything he told me concerned incidents on an administrative level. Incidents revealing his personal courage I had to learn about from other sources.

Though he only held the rank of Captain, Fiorello was frequently the medium of communication between the Italian Government and the American high command. At least one event is of considerable historical importance: shortly after his arrival on the Italian front the Austrian army, spearheaded by crack Prussian assault troops, started a terrific drive which was to result in the great rout at Caporetto. The Italian Army reeled back to the Piave blew some kisses at a cemetery. Fiorello was utterly unperturbed; when they got back the Italian pilot volunteered the explanation that it had just been a little gesture to his dead brother, who was buried there. Fiorello said, "Tomorrow we must go back and drop a wreath." But the return trip was unnecessary: the Italian Air Force was satisfied that Fiorello had "moxie."

Fiorello and his command saw plenty of action, but, though his plane was riddled several times, Fiorello was never hit. The American force was augmented, and he went on a number of bombing raids. The Austrians retaliated with bombing raids on the Italian airdrome cities. One day a committee of neighboring peasants asked to see him at the command post. After some nervous and evasive hedging, the peasant leader suggested that if Fiorello would agree to stop bombing the Austrians, the Austrians might stop bombing back; at least it was an experiment worth making. Fiorello readily and heartily agreed; he said he would initiate his part of the experiment at once. The reason for his immediate acquiescence lay in the fact that the squadron had just been ordered out of that sector that very night. All hands were extremely gratified by Fiorello's cooperative attitude. His only regret was that he would never know the results of so novel and intriguing an experiment. He laughed uproariously when he told me of it.

Fiorello was absolutely devoted to his command, as, apparently, they were to him. Military aviation was still in its hedgehopper stage, and Fiorello's resourcefulness must have been taxed to the limit. But that, of course, was the wide-open kind of setup he liked best; it gave him a chance to innovate. Not all of his energies were expended health. At another time he insisted on being taken down in the sister ship of the ill fated submarine *S4*, whose sinking had generated a great public hue and cry. Whatever he observed on the run must have been indisputable evidence, because when he surfaced he told the American people that the Navy was completely exonerated.

Fiorello's lifetime devotion to aviation is easily understood: it represented the latest phase of the American pioneering spirit; it stood for Progress; it was dangerous and demanded a high degree of physical courage. His first contact with it dated from the days when he was counsel for an airplane company financed by small investors and headed by the aeronautical engineering genius Giuseppe Bellanca, the brother of labor leader August Bellanca, Sidney Hillman's strongest supporter. Within a couple of years he had learned to fly. When World War I came along, this fact, taken together with his linguistic abilities, resulted in his appointment as Commanding Officer of the U.S. Air Branch on the Italian-Austrian front.

I heard quite a lot from Fiorello about his war experiences, but almost everything he told me concerned incidents on an administrative level. Incidents revealing his personal courage I had to learn about from other sources.

Though he only held the rank of Captain, Fiorello was frequently the medium of communication between the Italian Government and the American high command. At least one event is of considerable historical importance: shortly after his arrival on the Italian front the Austrian army, spearheaded by crack Prussian assault troops, started a terrific drive which was to result in the great rout at Caporetto. The Italian Army reeled back to the Piave

River. General Cadorna, Italian Chief of Staff, was relieved from duty, a very drastic step indeed, and General Diaz was sent in. When things were at their worst, Nitti, who was the Big Gun of the Italian cabinet, came to Fiorello and told him that Italy was on the ropes and about to go down for the count unless American aid came rapidly. This was the official position; he was speaking for the King and the Prime Minister. Would Fiorello board a fast Italian cruiser immediately and take this personal message to Wilson? Fiorello, quite properly, declined, and instead reported the request through channels to the American Ambassador. General Diaz then repeated the request, whereupon Fiorello went up to Chaumont to see General Pershing. Pershing hadn't earned his nickname of "Black Jack" for nothing. He simply reiterated that position which is now the dictum of the American Army: we fight as units and not as reserves for other armies. But help would be coming, Pershing said.

President Wilson, when notified, took the matter in hand himself. He sent personal orders to the Embassy for Captain La Guardia. The Commander-in-Chief instructed the Captain to pick a spot of his own choosing, and make a full-dress public speech. He was to tell the people of Italy that America was in the war to the finish, and that aid would be forthcoming to the beleaguered peninsula. Captain La Guardia was to use his own discretion, but he was instructed that any risk was justified to keep Italy in the war. Having charged the young Captain with this vast responsibility, Wilson provided an escape hatch for himself. "The orders ended," Fiorello said, "with this sentence: 'If you succeed, the American Government will endorse you; if you fail, you will be disavowed.' " That meant a censure severe enough to result in Fiorello's dismissal from the Army.

Fiorello picked the Genoa Stock Exchange for his speech, and it was a lulu. I have heard from other people that as he talked he seemed to grow from a man into an Alp, and that he swept all before him as he thundered to his conclusion. I have also heard it said that, at the end of his plea, with his arms outstretched in supplication, he collapsed dramatically across the podium, but this I decline to believe. All are agreed, however, that it was a great and historic speech. For the next few days Fiorello was rushed around Italy making other speeches, including one full-dress affair at La Scala, whose historic boards had been trod by artists of far less histrionic ability. Going from there to Rome, he carried America's fighting spirit to the Colosseum itself; and the people of Rome, their own fighting spirit aroused, gave him an ovation in the tradition of the Caesars. The original idea of using a young captain as his spokesman, speaking in Italian, is not always credited to Wilson, but it is true.

Pershing's answer to Diaz was to order the American Air Squadron, with Fiorello in command, to the front. His diplomatic mission accomplished, Fiorello rushed his squadron off to Padua, where he was already held in high regard by the aviators of the Italian Air Force. While waiting for planes from the U.S. to arrive, the Italian pilots decided to play a practical joke on him. He was invited on a reconnaissance flight, and when they were directly over an Austrian battery the Italian pilot dove sharply into the fire and, as they pulled out and started to climb again, blew some kisses at a cemetery. Fiorello was utterly unperturbed; when they got back the Italian pilot volunteered the explanation that it had just been a little gesture to his dead brother, who was buried there. Fiorello said, "Tomorrow we must go back and drop a wreath." But the return trip was unnecessary: the Italian Air Force was satisfied that Fiorello had "moxie."

Fiorello and his command saw plenty of action, but, though his plane was riddled several times, Fiorello was never hit. The American force was augmented, and he went on a number of bombing raids. The Austrians retaliated with bombing raids on the Italian airdrome cities. One day a committee of neighboring peasants asked to see him at the command post. After some nervous and evasive hedging, the peasant leader suggested that if Fiorello would agree to stop bombing the Austrians, the Austrians might stop bombing back; at least it was an experiment worth making. Fiorello readily and heartily agreed; he said he would initiate his part of the experiment at once. The reason for his immediate acquiescence lay in the fact that the squadron had just been ordered out of that sector that very night. All hands were extremely gratified by Fiorello's cooperative attitude. His only regret was that he would never know the results of so novel and intriguing an experiment. He laughed uproariously when he told me of it.

Fiorello was absolutely devoted to his command, as, apparently, they were to him. Military aviation was still in its hedgehopper stage, and Fiorello's resourcefulness must have been taxed to the limit. But that, of course, was the wide-open kind of setup he liked best; it gave him a chance to innovate. Not all of his energies were expended on behalf of aviation during the war, however. Even so large a field as that could hardly contain Fiorello's capacity for imaginative activity. One of his orders he regarded as nothing short of a milestone in military medicine, for instance. He had developed an idea, he said with some bitterness, which everybody else had copied since without giving him the slightest credit. To understand the importance of Fiorello's generously anonymous contribution, it is necessary to realize that the bane of pre-penicillin armies was venereal disease. In terms of combat effectiveness it was more of a problem than enemy artillery. Fiorello, pondering as to how it could best be fought, came up with a remarkable approach: he arranged for portable prophylactic stations to follow his men into the red-light districts. The stations themselves were marvels of inconspicuous simplicity, consisting of an enlisted man pushing a baby carriage in which were concealed the preventive medicines. It was all very unobtrusive to everyone but his troops, who knew what the baby carriage was for. Fiorello said that the whole thing had been a great success; he intimated that the Surgeon General was ready to commit hara-kari because he hadn't thought of it himself.

Once he had a terrific showdown with Pershing's headquarters, he told me; had he lost the argument, he said it would have resulted in his court-martial. The circumstances were these: the United States had placed a half-billion-dollar order with a certain Italian warplane manufacturer. The plane was a flying coffin, according to Fiorello; it killed his American test pilot. Fiorello promptly wired the factory, canceling the order, and within minutes he received instructions to report to American Headquarters in

Chaumont, France. Both Rome and Washington were quivering with rage.

It was Top Brass that he was ordered to report to. "I knew all hell would break loose, and it did," said Fiorello. "When I walked in, the general barely returned my salute, and he kept me standing at attention for several minutes. He was sore as a boil. He said, 'Just who the hell do you think you are, Captain? Where the hell did you get the authority to cancel a $500,000,000 order?' I looked him right in the eye and said, 'By virtue of the power in me vested to protect the lives of my men.' The general turned a fine shade of apoplectic red and shouted, 'I've got a God-damn' good mind to kick you out of the Army.' And I said: 'I wish you would. I'd like to go back to Congress and investigate the Army for buying those planes in the first place.' The general backtracked immediately, and asked how bad they were. I told him they were impossible. As it turned out I was sustained. The planes weren't used and no more were manufactured: out went the contract." Before Fiorello went back to Italy, a Headquarters spokesman suggested—in order to mollify what might be an investigating Congressman—that there might be a place for him on the General Staff. "I told him," said Fiorello grandly, "that I hadn't come all that distance to be insulted!"

The story behind one incident Fiorello carried to his grave. Italy was feeling the pinch of the submarine war in the Atlantic, and Nitti told Fiorello that Italy was running out of steel and, even worse, of tungsten. But there was a good deal of it in Spain. Fiorello said he duly reported the conversation to Headquarters, and was promptly ordered to Paris. He took along Albert Spalding, the great violinist, as his aide. At a secret conference the United States Treasury was put at the disposal of the two young officers, and they were ordered into Spain dressed as civilians. Fiorello and Spalding appeared not long thereafter off the breakwater in Genoa with four vessels loaded to the waterline with the precious metals. British Intelligence had had a lot to do with it, Fiorello said, but the man who was chiefly responsible for the coup had made it a condition that his name never be mentioned, and the details never revealed. Fiorello made a great point of the fact that it had been a very tricky business, a matter of state, and it was a matter of personal honor with him that the secret die with him. I was very impressed at the time, but having been a cloak-and-dagger bucko myself in the last war, the situation doesn't seem quite so spectacular now. In fact, if word got around that the U.S. Treasury was at anybody's disposal, I can easily imagine cabinet officials of a lot of other countries besides Spain forming a line to his right. Anyway, Fiorello delivered the goods.

That wasn't Fiorello's first or last Intelligence mission. He told me of an episode toward the end of hostilities which throws considerable light on how differently war is waged now. He had been a Consul in Hungary when he was very young, and so it was perhaps logical that word would be sent to him in Italy that a revolution was possible in Hungary, *if* the U.S. would support it.

Fiorello went to Switzerland to find out more, and what he found out was important and valid enough to wire encoded details to Secretary of State Lansing, with a request for instructions. "Lansing wired back," said Fiorello, "that he was shocked. He said we were engaged in making war, not revolutions. Can you imagine *that?*" (Times have certainly changed; today Lansing's nephews, Allen and John Foster Dulles, might be expected to view with equanimity any mass upheaval behind the Iron Curtain.)

Fiorello's war service was recognized by several medals. His only mention of them to me was in connection with an anecdote involving the King of Italy and D'Annunzio. The King was presenting the medals, and apparently there was some kind of reception before the event. D'Annunzio entered and joined the group around the King and Fiorello. Some kind remarks were made about Fiorello's war speeches, and in an attempt to be humorous Fiorello said to the King: "It isn't fair, Your Majesty. When D'Annunzio expands the language, people say he has coined a word, and call it poetry. If I do the same thing, they say its bad Italian, and barbarous slang." Fiorello said the King laughed, but D'Annunzio was inexplicably annoyed. Fiorello also said he told the King that monarchies were through. Surprisingly, the King agreed with him.

After Fiorello received his commission as Major, and for the rest of his life, he was called that by most of his friends and associates. In the office, we always referred to him as the "Major" or, more intimately, the "Maje."

After the war Fiorello's interest in aviation became, if possible, intensified. He was in the thick of the Billy Mitchell controversy, heatedly supporting Mitchell's thesis that the air age was not only here to stay but that air power was the country's chief military weapon of offense and defense. Fiorello swarmed all over Congress, stirring up interest and agitation over Mitchell's court-martial in 1925. Somehow or other he contrived to appear before the court-martialing board itself long enough to deliver a fiery tirade, at the conclusion of which one senior general, stimulated by the sulphurous atmosphere, was constrained to question the propriety of Fiorello's statements to the press. "Are you quoted correctly in the newspapers, sir," he growled, "in calling me nothing but a beribboned dog robber?"

"No, sir," snapped Fiorello, glaring back at him. "I was not aware you had any ribbons."

It is just possible that Fiorello's fierce defense of Mitchell against the Army brass was inspired to a certain small extent by the memory of his boyhood on Army posts as the son of an enlisted man. In those days the gulf between officers and men was almost medievally unbridgable. But his primary motivation in the Mitchell case was unquestionably his burning faith in the future of aviation.

His unswerving affection for aviation was matched by his implacable hostility toward the railroads. When a huge new railroad terminal, the very last word in transportation, opened on the West Side, Fiorello was the last person in the world who should have been invited to speak at the dedication ceremonies, but he was, and I dug up some material on the history of railroading for the occasion. Considering the magnitude of the event, I thought it only proper to stress the huge role the railroads had played in developing the country. I went eloquently to town on the twin lines of steel which united the nation, calling them at once both the skeleton and the nerve system of America. As Fiorello read all this, I could see he was taking a very dim view of it. He sniffed and snorted, and finally asked me if I was crazy. He said he certainly was not going to say that Vanderbilt, Hill, or Morgan had done anything good for the country; they had just been out for themselves; in fact, Commodore Vanderbilt had admitted as much. Also, they had corrupted the U.S. Senate, and now, fifty years later, he, Fiorello, wasn't going to "front" for a bunch of bandits. Furthermore, he continued, railroads were out, finished, and he just didn't know how to tell the poor fellows that their vast new terminal was obsolete before it had even opened.

The actual speech which he delivered wasn't much less extreme than his remarks to me had been; he complimented the railroad men in outrageous fashion on their coming part—in the Air Age! He congratulated them on their splendid new structure which, he estimated, would shortly be receiving a thousand helicopter boxcars a day. He made it sound as though a fleet of flying freight trains were due to arrive on the roof at any minute. The response of his audience to this glowing picture was less than enthusiastic.

Fiorello's affection for aviation was indiscriminate and general, but he was especially fond of pilots. He regarded them all as comrades-in-arms, part of a great freemasonry of the skies. The only pin I ever saw him wear was the QB of the Quiet Birdmen. It was owing to his passionate loyalty to his brethren of the clouds that a large part of U.S. Aviation Law reads as it does today. Fighting for his skymen, Fiorello was obliged to sanction the consolidation of the big airplane companies, since they were the only ones capable of meeting his wage demands. Even so, the big companies required the assistance of the U.S. Treasury. Commercial aviation in those days was like a butterfly just breaking out of its chrysalis. Fiorello hovered over it with tender hands, though from his speeches one would have gathered that aerial argosies were just over the horizon. The industry, though in its infancy, was a powerful baby, starting to kick the sides out of its crib. In spite of the depression, little airlines sprang up all over the country, some of them running from nowhere to nowhere, and others running from somewhere to halfway to somewhere else. The planes were mostly the old tri-motored Tin Geese and Curtis Condors, a biplane whose wings were still made of lacquered silk. Passengers sat in bucket seats and earned deserved reputations for being very advanced and daring. Publicity men hopefully distributed thousands of pictures of "regular" flights landing here and there, with everybody trying desperately to look casual. When one Chicago-bound plane crashed, the company pointed out that it was only fifty miles short of its goal.

But the little lines soon began to run from somewhere to somewhere: St. Louis to Chicago, Chicago to Detroit, and so on. Furthermore, these little lines were actually operating at a profit, because they were paying their pilots next to nothing. The regular lines couldn't compete without doing the same, and the pilots struck. That's where Fiorello came in. The pattern of air transportation in America was being cut, and Fiorello was right there with the scissors to see that his pilots got their share. In a very recent airplane pilot strike, it was revealed—and not questioned— that a skyliner's captain earns better than $18,000 a year. In my opinion, at least half of that paycheck is due to Fiorello's success in establishing the idea that the senior pilot must be considered the equal of the captain of an ocean liner. Fiorello harped on that endlessly after one of the embryo air tycoons had defined pilots as nothing but truck drivers of the sky.

The big fight on the status of pilots made the nation's headlines. It had the nostalgic ring of the twenties to it; at least here was some business worth fighting about, at a time when giving the country back to the Indians, provided they assume the carrying charges, would have seemed another outrageous swindle. At any rate, the headlines played it to the hilt. Fiorello's office was packed with striking aviators. They were led by Bert Acosta, that colorful and handsome man who had flown the Atlantic for Admiral Byrd. He had something of a reputation as a playboy, and there was an air of harmless mischief about him, but at the same time he was pleasantly diffident, and I thought he looked startled when Fiorello expatiated on the mayhem he was going to wreak on the "enemy." The fight, of course, was right down Fiorello's alley. It was on behalf of Progress, and against "Them." He would snarl to the assembled airmen: "When I get through with these leeches, they'll know their places. The pilot of an airplane is *not* a truck driver; he's the captain of a ship and I'll see that that's the way he's paid." There was a faint cheer, but I don't think any of the boys really believed he could do it.

As usual, though, Fiorello knew what he was about. Suddenly it was all over, like a naval battle. In fact, Fiorello's attack reminded me of the weight of the Atlantic Fleet's broadside squarely straddling some old Spanish fort like Morro Castle: just a great cloud of dust, and nothing else to be seen when it settled. The quick victory wasn't hard to explain. What Fiorello had done, of course, was to threaten the life line of all the air companies: they couldn't exist without subsidies through mail pay. Very well, no pilot pay, no subsidy. Q.E.D. For the marginal little companies who proposed to operate on a profit based on low pilots' pay came a mass of official regulations on safety and pilot qualifications which made their county-fair aviators ineligible for certification. In Fiorello's book these shoestring outfits weren't run by small businessmen at all; they were run by chiselers and vultures, ready to take a profit on human life. It always had to be black and white.

There were a few fitful flashes from the aviation companies as from a marsh after a swamp fire, but these swiftly subsided. Fiorello walked around for a while like a stiff-legged young lion licking his chops and pining for more dinner, but negative numbers are restricted to mathematics and in the everyday world there is nothing less than zero. He had not only won, he had annihilated, and there was nothing more to it. The pilots were in.

Shortly thereafter, Fiorello was flying out West, the better to breathe hotly down the neck of a certain Federal Judge. En route, his plane turned over in landing; although badly shaken up, he brushed the accident off as nothing and continued his trip—by plane. He would have done so had he lost a leg; Fiorello wouldn't even let Fiorello stand in the way of Progress.

He displayed the same zeal for aviation when he was Mayor. He insisted that the city put up an airport—and the multimillion-dollar project in Flushing Meadows resulted. The papers doubted the wisdom of it at the time. The *Sun* even called it La Guardia's Folly. But a year after it opened, its traffic was at saturation point, and the time came when another, much bigger one had to be built. To aviators, however, New York means La Guardia field. The great airport of the world's largest city is well named.

X

International affairs were of absorbing interest to Fiorello. Naturally enough, Italy was a special preoccupation; I remember very clearly how scathing he always was in his references to Mussolini, whom he considered a pitiful caricature of a man, a local barbershop bully involved in a game far beyond his capacities. He was convinced that Mussolini was a mere puppet whose strings were manipulated by the International Bankers. Never once did Fiorello credit him with being the head of a State. On the contrary, he used to ridicule the strutting little "sawdust Caesar," as though he were of no more real consequence than a ward heeler, a bargain-basement Pagliacci, the prisoner of Italy's short-term financial obligations.

On the general question of international financial obligations, which vexed both the twenties and the thirties, Fiorello had neither doubts nor qualms. He was for wiping them out, on the ground that it was downright silly to think in terms of ever collecting. He often pointed out that he had voted for foreign loans as a war measure and on condition that it be noted in the *Record* that he never expected

repayment. He spoke, I always thought, with solid authority on matters of international finance: he was an expert on
money and he had a realistic view of the productive potential of the European peoples. To put it baldly, he simply
took the position that you couldn't get blood from a turnip,
so why waste time trying?

The big crisis on the world front while I was in Fiorello's
office came when the Japanese drove into Shanghai. Fiorello flew into action. He called Secretary of State Stimson
at once and found the Secretary in complete accord with his
views. They remained in close touch for weeks. Stimson
was ready to accept war to stop the aggression; and Fiorello himself was for forcing war then and there. He took
steps to brush off his commission and prepared to go back
into the Army. He told me I could go with him. Meanwhile, he formulated plans to go to Shanghai himself as
soon as possible. The Chinese Route Armies were putting
up a good fight, and Fiorello thought that with reserves
thrown in they could win. The pressure was terrific; the
office was like a sand-hog chamber.

One afternoon the story broke that American women
and children were marooned in Shanghai. Fiorello responded like Man o' War spurred with a white-hot iron.
He was on the phone to Stimson within minutes of getting
the news. The Fleet! Where the hell was the Fleet? Send
it in! The Marines! Land the Marines! Get those women
and children out of there! Action, God damn it! Action!

Stimson called back and told him that a cruiser had
cleared Manila for Shanghai under forced draught. Fiorello asked about the Marines, and roared with disgust on
being told that there were only seventy-two aboard, plus a

band. But, in the event, these few proved to be enough.

Knowing the U.S. Marines to be my major enthusiasm (in any discussion of appropriations I always urged an increase for them), Fiorello asked me after it was all over if I wanted to see a special showing of the newsreel pictures in full of the Marines conducting American women and children out of Shanghai. I leaped at the chance. I still think it the most dramatic and moving thing I have ever seen. The Marine company was lined up in front of an Embassy building, looking like just what they are, cold and professional soldiers, the greatest organization of fighting men in the history of the world. The command was given to fix bayonets. The steel clattered home. Then followed a magnificent troop placement, considering the job at hand. Two squads in squad front, with two squads in reserve, formed the phalanx. The remaining squads were deployed down the sides as a rear echelon of two squads, thus forming a long rectangle. Into this stockade of men poured the women and children with all sorts of household paraphernalia, the women trying to carry their bundles and to hang onto their youngsters at the same time. They massed right behind the band, which in turn was immediately behind the colors, under double guard.

Then a major took up his position alone *in front* of the line of bayonets, drew his .45 and ordered the column forward. That may have been questionable military tactics according to the book, but it was magnificent military strategy, psychologically speaking. The band played "Semper Fidelis" and the whole shebang moved out, the women and children bobbing haphazardly within the walls of precisely synchronized graven images, their fixed bayonets at port arms. The frenzied crowd closed behind them, but it opened before them. As always, the Marines accomplished their mission with dispatch and spectacular éclat. As they moved past the British outposts, the Tommys jumped up on their sandbag barricades and cheered. It was the supreme accolade of one professional fighting group to another.

But if Stimson was ready to fight, the Great Engineer in the White House was not. As a matter of fact, the White House went out of its way to veto Fiorello's demands for action. However, much of what Fiorello called for came about. He had strongly suggested a concentration of naval power by all civilized nations, and one morning Shanghai awoke to find the Whangpoo a forest of battle tops: the British Far East Squadron was in. Simultaneously, the American Battle Fleet moved west out of San Diego. Things seemed to be picking up, but the White House let it be known that these were only routine Pacific fleet maneuvers that had been planned the year before.

The big diplomatic question centered on whether China's economic boycott was an act of aggression. A Commission was appointed to examine the facts. When Fiorello heard this, he acted as if he had been injected with ptomaine poisoning. The Commission studied on and on. British Foreign Secretary Sir John Simon said the situation deserved the most serious consideration. "Big news," groaned Fiorello. He said Simon was hedging. When it turned out that Simon's recommendation amounted to taking no action at all, Fiorello went to see Stimson, but he knew the fight was lost. When he came back, he threw the outline of a memorandum on my desk. It was Britain's refusal to force war at Shanghai. "Take a look at that, Ernest," he said with deepest bitterness. "And remember it. It's the death warrant of the British Empire—signed by Britain herself." However, he told me that the British were ready to back Stimson, but that they knew Stimson couldn't deliver the President and the Congress, which would have left them high and dry with a war on their hands. As it worked out, Stimson finally forced the Japanese to modify their position because of the immense world reaction against them.

During all this period the tension in the office was so heavy it was almost unbearable. Everyone was subdued and strained, like a group of relatives waiting for the result of major surgery in a hospital sitting room. The Major would come charging out like a hurricane, and we would scatter before him like grazing gazelles before a charging lion. Then he would be gone, and we'd reassemble, so to speak. Then he'd be in again, and again we'd fly. Fiorello was reliving his brilliant World War I days. He became gruff and military. He called me "Captain" quite seriously, and this suited me fine, since ordinarily I would have been too young to be anything but a shavetail. I hoped, if we were going into actual battle, he could make the Captaincy stick.

But the inevitable comic relief had to come. The fourth desk in the office was occasionally occupied by Nick Saldiveri, who handled Veterans' affairs. Nick had a high bald dome and tufts of mouse-brown hair which stuck out on the sides of his head, giving him a definitely Dickensian look. His appearance was not tidy; as often as not he needed a shave. He was a conscientious fellow, and always treated American Legion matters as if they were affairs of State of the first magnitude. He affected a confidential air when talking about his work, as if it were a great privilege for us to be let in on such important matters. To emphasize his busyness, he often wore a pencil behind his ear, which reminded me of nothing so much as a butcher boy. But the officious externals weren't the real Nick. He was kind, one of the kindest men I ever knew, and everybody loved him. His was the soul of a cocker spaniel.

Nevertheless, when the Shanghai incident broke, something went off in Nick. World War I had been the big event in his life, and now he smelled another big adventure. We had to defer to him because he had had military experience, and we hadn't. He straightened up and became slightly fierce, which was mildly comic, for he was middle-aged and had a noticeable little potbelly. But Nick squared his shoulders like a Scots Grey dragoon sniffing distant gunpowder, and there he sat, his nostrils distended all day long.

When we heard that the Major was going to Shanghai, Nick quietly disappeared. The next thing we knew, the door opened, and back came Nick, struggling with a mountain of military paraphernalia—knapsacks, mess kits, bedrolls, everything. There just wasn't room for it all in the office. But out he went again, and in came more stuff. The final effect was impressive; the place looked like Cain's Theatrical Warehouse.

"Shanghai," he said to Mimi in brief and unnecessary explanation, as he dusted his hands on his trousers.

It would have been fine if the orders to go to Shanghai had come in just then. But they didn't, nor did they ever. At just about this point Fiorello decided he could go faster and more effectively as a diplomat than as a military man, and the Army atmosphere eased up. No longer was I called "Captain," but I bore this philosophically. On the other hand there was Nick, primed to explode but minus the fuse. The sudden lifting of tension demanded a release from us all, and poor Nick provided just the material we needed. Mimi composed an ode in heroic couplets commemorating Nick's heroic preparations for the relief of Shanghai, and we went into paroxysms of helpless laughter. Nick grinned sheepishly, taking it all with characteristic good nature; but once or twice I saw him shoot Fiorello a look full of gentle reproach.

Though he admired and supported Secretary Stimson's strong Far East policy, Fiorello distrusted the motives of the State Department. He believed that the Interests were in there, as the phrase goes, four deep in every position, and that Dollar Diplomacy was a scandalously strong factor in State Department decisions. At the time of the Shanghai invasion, a young American editor there was publishing a sheet which was giving the State Department a severe migraine. His publication was protested by either the Japanese or the Chinese, I forget which, and the State Department disavowed him, saying that anything he printed was on his own hook and at his own risk. So far so good, but the situation couldn't remain static. The next issue of the newspaper must have been a scorcher, because the international repercussions were terrific. Now State let it be known it was picking up the young editor's passport. Fiorello at once demanded to know by what authority the State Department could pick up any American's passport. At that time no such authority existed. Fiorello raised such a fuss about it that Stimson himself took over. He explained that

State wasn't really taking up the passport; they were merely depriving the young editor of the "higher diplomatic protection." Fiorello pounced on that one like a terrier on a rat. Just what was this "higher diplomatic protection," he wanted to know. He had spent a lifetime trying to find out, he said. He guessed he had been misled by the Constitution and the Declaration of Independence, which stated that all men were equal before the law. Now just what "higher diplomatic protection" were the big U.S. business firms getting in Shanghai that that boy wasn't? It was imperative that these things be defined, etc., etc.

The upshot of all this was that not only did the "boy" stay, but his very attractive young wife was given special dispensation to go out and join him. She came in to see Fiorello shortly thereafter, and they had quite a talk. Fiorello was deeply touched. "She said," he told me, "that they were both in my debt. She cried like a little girl." He sighed happily.

"Well," I said, "you aren't going to let her go, are you?"

"Certainly I am," he replied, puzzled. "Why not?"

"In the first place," I said, "she might get hurt, and in the second place what the hell can she do to help him?"

"Listen," rumbled Fiorello, "if we can send a cruiser to Buenos Aires to bring *out* Pittsburgh Plate Glass, we can send a young wife *in* to her husband. Besides, I think it's splendid of her to stand by her husband and want to be with him in his hour of need. That's Youth for you!"

The Department of State was on more than one occasion beset by the fidgets where Fiorello was concerned. During his career as Mayor of New York he gave the diplomatic brass in Washington more than one restless night, for, as

Mayor, Fiorello would often be the first to greet visiting foreign V.I.P.'s who were using New York as their port of entry. The representatives of countries in his favor got red-carpet treatment, but those from governments of which he happened to disapprove were liable to be given excessively short shrift, not to say the brush-off. When Fulgencio Batista, the Cuban dictator, was due to arrive in New York on a formal visit to the United States, the State Department held its breath. Suggestions regarding the proper protocol were hesitantly tendered to Fiorello, but he waved them aside with his usual imperious air. In rejecting these pointers he managed to intimate that the duly elected Chief Magistrate of the City of New York needed no gratuitous advice from mere appointees who had never won their spurs from an electorate. Chagrined, the State Department withdrew but asked somewhat piteously if they might not be kept informed. To this Fiorello magnanimously agreed.

The two men met at the airport. Within seconds they were on the friendliest possible terms, laughing and patting each other on the back. Torn between relief and curiosity, the State Department afterward asked Fiorello about the spontaneous sympatico that had arisen between him and Batista. Fiorello blandly explained that he had established an immediate bond with his first words of greeting. Which were? "Hi, Sergeant, have a good five-cent cigar!"

Many years later, as head of UNRRA, this same calculatedly slapdash ebullience of his saved precious weeks and miles of red tape in a critical situation. Cotton was needed—a very substantial quantity of it. Peru, he was told, had cotton for sale. The State Department agreed that negotiations should be initiated through the usual channels for the purchase of Peruvian cotton. This was too slow for Fiorello, though; he wanted the cotton at once. He got it, too—by dint of some close horse trading via long distance with the President of Peru, Manuel Prado y Ugarteche. Diplomatic protocol went out the window as Fiorello opened the conversation with, "Hello, Manny? Listen—"

XI

Politics has been described as the Art of the Possible as applied by the Science of the Second-Best. Churchill calls it the most difficult of the arts, and it is certainly no small task to extract harmony from a whole chorus of dissonant and strident voices, few of which are even working on the same song. But Fiorello, from his basso profundo attacks to his C above high C supplicando tremolo, could match anybody's tune, from Nicholas Murray Butler's clarion call to international cooperation to Hymie Schorenstein's wail that you didn't have to be literate to be Kings County Register. I read an account once of Foch, after the war, comparing notes with his principal opponent, Von Hindenburg. In the same spirit Fiorello often conversed with his political enemies. In the old-school tradition, a flag of truce for communication was never violated, and a word given was never broken. Unfortunately, this noble tradition died in the bloodletting over the New Deal. But up to that time it was honored, and Theodore Roosevelt spoke warmly of it. When Boss Quay died, T.R. called in Lincoln Steffens and sternly told him that the reformers didn't

know a good man when they saw one. Quay, on his death-
bed, had called for his arch-opponent, Roosevelt, and
asked him to take care of an Indian tribe he sponsored.
Having fought Teddy, he had learned to trust him.
Fiorello inspired the same feeling in his opponents; it is
noteworthy that he had the endorsement of Ogden Mills,
who must have hated, in the vernacular, his guts. And Nicholas Murray Butler, though he must have shrunk at the
thought of the sweaty political scuffles into which Fiorello
unhesitatingly plunged, nevertheless endorsed him heartily. Similarly, the Tammany leaders who knew Fiorello
best, and who also knew every trick in the political grab
bag, treated him with utmost consideration even as the
public laughed at him for his jeremiads. As practical politicians, they knew he knew the truth, and they feared him.
Jimmy Hines alone demonstrated his inability to get the
point. He was later able to regret his hasty judgment in en-
forced leisure.

Watching Fiorello in action was sheer nourishment for a
young man looking for an education in political know-
how. Anybody can get on with anybody else, but to watch
someone do it without compromise, being at the same time
the focal point of crucial issues—that is something else
again. Fiorello's basic approach was rugged, almost trucu-
lent. He always led from strength. "You can't help it if
they don't like you," he once said to me, "but you can com-
pel them to respect you." From the White House to Dutch
Schultz's headquarters, he was respected as a Two-Gun
Man.

Part of this was due to his prescience. He said to me
more than once, "I'll tell you what they are saying right

now"—and then proceeded to give me an account of a conversation that would prove to be uncannily accurate. I remember one instance particularly well. Fiorello said: "Kingsland Macy is telling the President he can handle me. (He can't.) Hoover is telling him that he doubts it. Macy is telling Hoover it deserves a try and Hoover agrees. The first thing, Macy says, is to convince me I haven't been read out of the Party. So he'll offer me some patronage." Sure enough, Macy did just that, in the Immigration Department. What happened thereafter provided me with considerable food for thought. Fiorello decided to accept the patronage on the ground that it was a sensitive job requiring the services of the best possible man. No one could disagree with that. On the basis of the public interest, and on that basis alone, Fiorello was prepared to assist in combing the field. He named two candidates, one of whom got the job. It was abundantly clear that Fiorello had collected the patronage but that he was under no obligation whatsoever; he had named his conditions of public service, and his nomination came strictly under that head. To do that, inside a party, you have to be good. Fiorello was.

On the other hand, Fiorello could condone the seamier aspects of local politics when there was no help for it. A voter once asked Fiorello if a certain Republican leader deserved support, and the answer, after adding up the pros and cons, was in the affirmative. As the voter was leaving, Fiorello remarked sarcastically that since this Republican leader was in the habit of throwing ten-dollar bills around, the voter should make sure he got his! That Fiorello knew every nuance and hidden pitfall of workaday politics cannot be doubted. Once when I was signing for election material Fiorello came out of the office and asked me what I was doing. I told him, and he said not to do it, that it made me personally liable, and he mentioned a City Court decision so holding.

It was from Fiorello that I first learned about "goldbricking"—or overt support to one candidate and covert support to another at the Election Day showdown. Fiorello said that goldbricking was a hard thing to detect and that he knew people who had been goldbricked and didn't know it to this day. Briefly, goldbricking is a political trade on a nomination, whereby A, a secret supporter of B, agrees to support C for three or four ballots, on condition that C agrees to support A's announced second choice, which is really his first choice B, if and when C finds he can't make it. All along A and B have a secret deal with D to stop C. In short, in return for C's vote they heartily endorse C, knowing he can't possibly win, and then in the end they finally use C's own vote to flatten him. Goldbricking accounts for the phenomenon in conventions that front runners seldom win: they get all the votes which remain neutral until the final winner starts to gain strength. Then they "jump the bandwagon." A second type of goldbricking occurs when the few leaders who know who is going to be nominated at first split and support a different candidate to pay off a previous obligation to him. Fiorello said that the Republicans always tried to goldbrick him in the Party councils; it was, he said, the normal payoff for "liberals." But, unlike others, Fiorello always knew what was going on.

The anatomy of Fiorello's political philosophy was based on the individual voter in his district. The election was the pay-off, and on it everything depended. All Congressmen accept this; it is an axiom that the best speech on the Floor isn't worth one answered letter to a constituent, in so far as survival in office is concerned. Fiorello's mail was thoroughly answered, and the most accurate files were kept. The mass of detail, however, was handled by the competent staff, and only extra-routine matters came to Fiorello's personal attention.

There was in Fiorello's district a curious semi-club known as the Ghiboneys, half clown and half bully boys, who were uncritically devoted to Fiorello. They were not unlike the early New York City volunteer firemen of a hundred years before, being long on gusto, in boisterous good health, and anxious to plunge into any fray offering good clean fun. Fiorello paid little or no attention to them except in the election season, but they were invaluable as organizers and guards during the actual contest. They were, in a sense, Fiorello's Minute Men.

While the personal contact was carefully nurtured, Fiorello's main concern was policy. He took definite positions and was at great pains to state his reasons for them. These reasoned arguments he forcibly brought to the attention of his district's voters, paying them the compliment of assuming they had a brain in their respective heads and cared about the issues of the day. This paid dividends; his constituents appreciated him and were proud of him. Local pride is a familiar feature in American politics: Idaho was always proud of the national reputation of Borah, Arkansas of Robinson, Mississippi of Harrison, Alabama of Underwood and Bankhead, and so on. Election districts always basked in the reflected glory of representatives who were national leaders. Fiorello enjoyed a great deal of this feeling in the Twentieth: the Little Flower was a Big Man. But he never forgot to value every vote as though it were a marquise emerald. There is a certain inexorable mathematical progression behind this that is the very essence of ward contests. Each vote switched is two votes lost: one you lose and one your opponent gains; it therefore takes three votes to beat one switch.

Fiorello's relationship with the Republican Party leadership couldn't have existed had it not been the unwritten division of power which existed in New York for years. The Republicans got the national offices, the Democrats the city, and it was anybody's ball game in the state. The Republican leaders got the insurance, the Democratic leaders the contracts. The Republicans got trotting, the Democrats horseracing. Obviously, the Democrats didn't want Fiorello camping out in their back yard; on the other hand, Fiorello in Washington was theoretically boxed by the Republican majority. This held true during most of the twenties, but the sides of the box fell apart in 1929 and Fiorello was all over the lot after that.

His relationships with Congressional colleagues was, with but few exceptions, warm and friendly. He had objectives he wanted to accomplish, and his best course was to persuade his colleagues that he was right. Only if he had to did he offer vinegar to flies. But in or out of harmony with his brethren in the House, he enjoyed every minute he spent in Washington.

1932 was an election year for Fiorello, and he took it very seriously indeed. Tension started to mount along about March. No frenzy, but there was the remorseless calendar, moving up like a growing breeze from another quarter, a breeze that would eventually and inevitably swell to hurricane proportions.

I noticed the prevalence of a certain camaraderie among even opposed Congressmen in the common crisis they faced. Some of the Alabama Congressmen had told Fiorello they were in something of a pickle because of their support of the Sales Tax. With great good humor he told them to put his name up in big letters and to tell their audiences that they wanted anybody who could even pronounce it to vote against them! He said his name had too many vowels for Alabama consumption, and that such a gambit would be sure-fire. As a matter of strict fact, he thought the name Fiorello cost him 10,000 votes in every New York election. Whether the Alabamans took his advice I am sorry to say I do not know; but it gave Fiorello a hearty laugh to suggest it to them.

As the spring of 1932 began to loosen winter's grip, Fiorello talked more and more about the coming election, and sometimes, usually at the end of an especially tense and hectic day, he would reminisce about past elections. I particularly remember one story of an earlier campaign when he had run from a District which encompassed an area that included a very heavy Jewish population in one section of the District and a large upper-class American Republican population in another section of the District. Fiorello's Democratic opponent was fighting a dirty fight, accusing Fiorello of being anti-Semitic. Fiorello decided to spike that lie once for all. He challenged his opponent to a debate at a synagogue forum and pounded at it until the man had to accept.

After they were on the platform, Fiorello specified a condition of the debate: it must be in Yiddish. Fiorello spoke Yiddish fluently, and he had, of course, discovered that his adversary couldn't speak it at all. His opponent went to bat with two strikes against him to begin with and proceeded to look at a third strike without even knowing it.

"Why," said Fiorello, "that poor boob didn't even know you keep your hat on in a synagogue. He took his off."

But his opponent wasn't finished. He had pictures of himself in a Jewish velvet hat and a beard distributed all over the East Side; but on the West Side he was pictured as clean-shaven and wore a smart small-knotted tie. Fiorello said he always deplored the spurious racial issue, but if that was the game the guy wanted to play, that was the game he was going to get. So Fiorello put out a lot of special crews who spent all of the night before election transferring the East Side pictures of the opposing candidate to the West Side and the West Side pictures to the East Side.

In another election, said Fiorello, some bird-brained Republican leaders made a deal without his knowledge that nearly cooked his goose. There was a Democratic primary fight on, and the challenging Democratic district leader told the Republican leader to pay no attention to the registration of the "ringers" he was bringing in from out of the district, as they wouldn't be voting in the election, but only in the Democratic primary. In any event, there was some sort of deal by which the Republicans did not challenge the phony registrations. On Election Day the big double cross took place. The ringers all showed up and voted against Fiorello, but their numbers were not enough to stop his

Two old campaigners

A day at the office

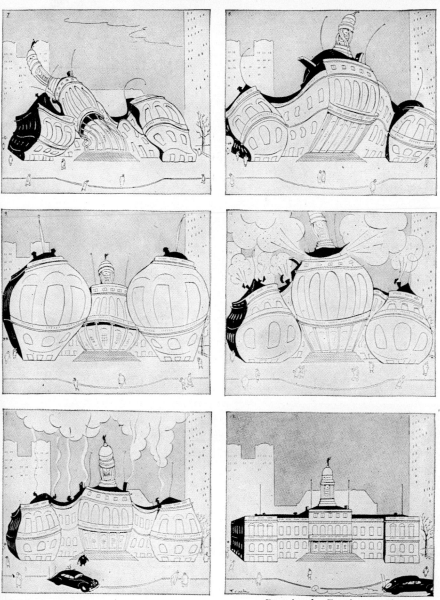

Drawing by Frueh, reproduced by permission. Copyright 1940 by The New Yorker Magazine, Inc.

Horseplay with
Eddie Rickenbacker

Consultation with his young D.A.

The friend of Generals

New York Press Photographers Association

Chess with Tito

The Maestro

The Critic

A fond farewell

landslide. Just the same, Fiorello made sure that *that* wouldn't ever happen again.

As the days lengthened, it was apparent that Fiorello intended to make political hay whenever and wherever possible. He called upon the Army to refuse plane deliveries because wages had been cut by the airplane companies; failing that, he tried to prevent the letting of new contracts without minimum-wage provisions. At the same time, he insisted that the Navy compete in the International Speed Races, this in the sacred name of Progress. The admirals replied that they'd be glad to, if someone would oblige by authorizing the money. Fiorello dropped the subject. He used to say that any given bill could be doomed for three reasons, the first of which was that there would be no appropriation, and that consequently the other two didn't matter.

Fiorello's precampaign maneuvers were textbook illustrations of nimble political footwork. He perceived that there would be a Democratic landslide in New York. He set out, therefore, to get the nominations of both major parties, and but for the stupidity of one man, Tammany's Jimmy Hines, he would have succeeded. Very shrewdly, Fiorello was trying a tack: that is to say, he intended using the very wind which was blowing against his nominal Party to elect him. To do this he intended to capitalize on his standing as the champion of the Progressives, and have the Progressives urge his nomination on the Democrats. The Democrats knew they needed the Progressives, but they did not know how much. The Progressives urged strongly, but they did not demand. A few years later and they might have; and a lot of history would have been written differently. As it was, their surge carried Fiorello up to the last barrier, Jimmy Hines, where it broke on his adamant refusal. John L. Lewis, William Green, and Senator Robert Wagner went heavily to bat for Fiorello; but Jimmy said No, and his was the decisive say at Tammany Hall. Not giving Fiorello that nomination which would have kept him in Washington was the worst mistake Hines ever made. Fiorello wanted desperately to go back to Congress, and it is my personal opinion that he would have made the greatest Speaker in American history. But it was not to be; Tammany, knuckling under Hines's pressure, wouldn't allow it. Having no place else to go, Fiorello later went to City Hall; and Jimmy Hines, in accordance with the findings of twelve good men and true, later went to Sing Sing.

No stone was left unturned—and, in a sense, unthrown —while the possibility of his election existed, however. Even John McCooey, the Brooklyn czar, was brought into it. Fiorello asked me to go to the Little Venice with him one night to meet McCooey, who looked like a prosperous pink-and-white little Santa Claus. Fiorello told him the problem and McCooey minced no words. He marveled at the stupidity of Hines. He said, in cultivated tones, "Mr. La Guardia, I assure you that my most difficult problem is to keep my Republican opposition in the running." I was entranced by the candor of this statement. McCooey impressed me as a man of large affairs, a real professional. He smiled when he said: "Mr. La Guardia, I'd like to see you made Ambassador to Australia; but, failing that, I'll try to send you back to Washington. Anywhere, so long as you're kept out of New York City."

Samuel Untermeyer was also canvassed. He was a smart lawyer, Fiorello observed, because among other things he always answered questions in Congressional investigations before his client could answer and thereby make a fool of himself. Fiorello was very anxious to have Untermeyer's support, and one night, while we were riding through Herald Square, he actually asked me in near anguish if I thought Untermeyer would "stand up." Apparently I wasn't reassuring enough, because Fiorello got very irritated with me. Untermeyer did stand up, but Jimmy Hines still refused to give an inch. Instead he put up a man by the name of Lanzetta, and the battle was joined. I think Fiorello knew his chances were slim without the Democratic sponsorship, but he collected his forces together for the best effort of which he was capable.

He made public-speaking appearances as often as possible. In the early fall of 1932 he accepted an invitation to speak at the Suffolk County Republican Club. I was invited to go. A big limousine called for us on the appointed night and in we got. The glass went up between us and the chauffeur. As it sealed us off Fiorello said grandly, as if announcing the Kellogg Pact or the Locarno Agreement, "I attached two conditions to speaking tonight." I asked what they were, expecting some kind of momentous horse trade. "One": said Fiorello expansively, "that they send a car to take me there and back, and two," he said with great emphasis, "number *two:* that the chauffeur not talk to me coming or going." The driver must in fact have been so instructed, for he never once opened his mouth. Fiorello acted as though the deal had been a very important personal triumph for him; I just nodded.

Miles out on Long Island we got out of the car in front of a low building set somewhat back from the road, a community house rather like an American Legion headquarters. A path led up to the door, and off to the right was a flagpole. A lot of people were assembled, and banks of bright lights were on. A bugle blew as we started up the path in the glare, and the crowd came to attention. Just as we were opposite the flagpole, a brass cannon went off about six feet from my ankles—or so it seemed. It sounded like the Krupp arsenal exploding, and as the flash and the brimstone simultaneously enveloped me I shied violently into Fiorello.

He never even flinched—just kept walking on and looking straight ahead, as if he hadn't heard or seen a thing. I recovered and fell into step with him again; but I could hear people laughing, and why not? As we were hanging up our coats, he said in a low voice: "That was a fine military spectacle you made of yourself. Why the hell didn't you tell me you were nervous about guns?" I said miserably I hadn't known I was, and apologized. He gave me his most withering glance, and I slunk off into a far corner.

They gave him a standing ovation when he had finished speaking, and the local bigwigs escorted us back to the car. I cast a wary eye over the greensward, but the brass cannon was gone. Fiorello sank back. We rode in silence for some time. I could tell that Fiorello was writhing with suppressed laughter, and suddenly he exploded. "*I* saw the god-damned cannon when we got out," he roared. "And I *knew* you were going to jump. But by God," he howled, "I didn't expect you to bolt!"

By and large, however, the atmosphere during this period was seldom alleviated by such light comedy. Fiorello had little campaign money; but, unlike the party machines, he did not consider this a matter of life or death. It was useful, even very useful, but if you didn't have it you had to do the best you could without it. What you did have to have was plenty of shoeleather; and Fiorello's volunteers canvassed every vote in the district. Fiorello was very finicky indeed about campaign contributions. He was very wary lest he be compromised in this direction, and took great precautions to see that everything was scrupulously on the up-and-up. I don't believe he ever saw a dollar which went into any of his campaigns; of one thing I am certain: he wanted not five cents' worth of help from the "Interests"—from "Them." In his first mayoralty campaign a year later, his campaign fund was absolutely broke. His staff was about to be evicted from its headquarters when in marched a bright young lieutenant with a check for $25,000—signed by the president of a big New York utility. La Guardia read the check, tore it in two, handed it back, and said, "Tell him I'd rather have my headquarters in the back of a Mack truck."

But to get back to the 1932 campaign: I was with him a great deal during the whole of it, and a more shrewd, knowing, intuitive, and consciously artful politician I never hope to see. There was always method to his madness, from grand strategy to a minor skirmish. The crux of his theory he once summed up for me in two sentences: "The tide of history sweeps the radical of today into the

Presidency of tomorrow. Kites rise against the wind."

I felt as though I were standing on the bridge with him, and that under the momentum of a rising gale the ship was beginning to bury her nose in the heavy mounting seas. I wasn't disappointed; the campaign was in every respect a political tornado.

XII

Fiorello's campaign had for me an epic quality of almost Homeric proportions. He made it seem that way. He dramatized every instant of it. He was the dauntless captain of a gallant, horribly beleaguered ship, and though we yawed on the very brink of eternity, because of his supreme skill and courage we did not go under.

It was theatrical; it was also quite genuinely awe-inspiring. Years later, standing on the top deck of the *Mauretania* as she battled with gale winds and a huge sea, the image struck me with fresh force; more than ever it seemed appropriate that I should have thought of that 1932 campaign in terms of a plunging vessel, monstrous waves, and heroic captain at the helm.

My services in the campaign were assumed. Bundles of ordered campaign literature arrived, and I signed for some. Fiorello told me not to do that because money was very limited; everything had to be checked in a central place. Otherwise, diversity of control would result in our buying things we couldn't pay for. He also told me that if I signed for anything I'd be liable, which was something to think about, too. It made me feel very uneasy, however, to see him concern himself about a $68 order when he was fighting for his political life.

Then Fiorello told me that in the campaign I was to be a speaker. Speaking on street corners is certainly nothing new in political campaigns. In fact, street-corner stumping sounded a little unattractive intrinsically, and I wondered if I might not be getting some kind of brush-off.

But it was nothing of the kind; quite the contrary. In Fiorello's district, it was an important position and an important trust—something like a squire moving up to knighthood, or a young Annapolis graduate getting his first command. It was more than a promotion; it was an elevation. Even the office began treating me as if I had been transmuted from lead into something approximating gold. At the time I could see neither rhyme nor reason to all this. It seemed to me that nobody ever paid much attention to political speakers in general, and even less to street-corner speakers in particular. I came to the conclusion that it was a Twentieth Congressional District folkway, a logic-tight compartment no more explicable than the Uganda ladies' custom of putting saucers in their lower lips or their European sisters' custom of putting diamonds in the lobes of their ears. However, as soon as I was aware of the prestige involved, I played it to the hilt and assumed the airs of a man of very considerable importance whose capabilities have belatedly but at last been recognized.

Fiorello said that my speaking would start any day now and to get ready. I asked him what he wanted me to talk about and he seemed a little surprised, and said, why, anything I pleased. The implication was that I was thoroughly conversant with the situation and could play the whole thing by ear. I was very pleased. Again I marveled at the parochial aspects of the custom. Such a compliment from the ordinarily deprecating Fiorello was as inwardly startling as suddenly being addressed respectfully by a colonel would be to a habitually browbeaten second lieutenant.

"Get together with Marc," Fiorello said, and waved me out. I felt fine.

Vito Marcantonio dropped into the office occasionally. He was an Assistant United States District Attorney. Fiorello, so the story went, had heard him deliver a ringing oration as a high-school student and had thereupon tucked him in that very draughty spot—under his wing. Marc was expected to check in with us that very day. He came, and was closeted with Fiorello. I buttonholed him as he was leaving and told him of my conversation with the Major. We walked down the corridor together.

Marcantonio's appearance in those days was unusual: he was slight of build, and since his feet were giving him some trouble he favored one leg. His hair was long, lank, and came over his forehead. His face was painfully thin, with very prominent cheekbones and sunken cheeks. This gave his jaw line a sharp, angular thrust. His eyes were large and intelligent, his mouth was large and his lips full. He had the Bourbon look of combined sensuousness and asceticism.

Marcantonio, since, has been regarded as a follower of the Communist Party line. Whatever his inclinations in this direction may have been—and I shared none of them—he was still one of the smartest cookies I ever encountered, one who could trade political punches blow for blow with any comer. He was a really tough guy.

I told him that the Major had asked me to speak, and asked if he had any suggestions as to what I should say. He said No, just give 'em hell, shoot the works, there was nothing to it, it was very simple. I asked to whom I should give the works, and he said that we took no guff from anybody.

"When George Medalie became D.A.," Marc said, "he called all of us young men in and said that he appreciated the party system which had brought us there, but that *that* took us only as far as the door. That's where the Republican Party ended. Inside, we were his employees, and he said he was an exacting boss. Well, I stepped right out and told him I'd got my job by working for the Party, just as he had, and I said I thought the reward in my case wasn't half enough."

It was clear that Marc regarded this as an act of great independence and courage, compelling the admiration of all fair-minded men. I wondered how the parable would help me to decide who not to take guff from. At the elevator he said we started the next night and to meet him at the F. H. La Guardia Club, uptown.

That night I started amassing and reviewing material relating to the failure of the City Trust Company. It was a small bank in Harlem which through the faithlessness of its officers had gone broke, losing all the savings of the people of small means in the district. Some of the bank's officials, incidentally, were active members of the Democratic Party in the district. They, I thought, would make a good Target for Tonight.

No one disturbed me the next day at the office; it was understood that I was Working on My Speech. I intended to join the F. H. La Guardia Club that night; indeed, it was taken for granted that I would, now that I had joined the shock troops.

What happened at the club that night is difficult for me to describe. There was a little room on the bottom floor, off the street, with ten or twelve men in it, and a small coffee urn on a counter. I didn't know any of the men there, but I was expected. They couldn't have been kinder, but it was painfully obvious that they did not regard me as one of them. After the first awkward moments, conversation came to a dead stop. When I essayed some very small talk, one spokesman would politely answer me. Everyone seemed frightfully ill at ease, myself most of all. I have an impression that we presently went to the second floor, where a typed application on ordinary newsprint was handed to me. I read the first paragraph, a sort of preamble which promised unconditional loyalty to the policies and leadership of Fiorello La Guardia, past, present, and future, in language which all but said Now and Forever, Amen. Sweat collected on my forehead. I fumbled for a handkerchief. I knew I couldn't sign it. Hell, I disagreed with Fiorello twice a day, and he didn't seem to mind at all. He would understand why I couldn't sign. I excused myself and went to Marc. I told him I wouldn't sign a declaration like that, not if it were for my own father. I felt anguished. Marc was breezy. "Well, forget it, for God's sake," he said. "If you don't want to sign it, don't sign it. Come on, let's get going. It's late." I felt very grateful to him. We left, and I never went back there again.

The Twentieth District ran from about 100th Street to somewhere up around 120th, and from Lexington Avenue over to the East River. Its heart was 116th Street. It encompassed at that time a large Italian and a considerable Puerto Rican population. It included many huge tenements, where yellow lights shone dimly from the backs of long dark corridors deep within. The black store windows of small ventures which had gone under stared out onto the shabby streets like empty eyeball sockets. Nearly all the buildings seemed insubstantial and oddly nightmarish, like the settings in the German movies being shown about that time. I was strongly reminded of old trees, not uprooted, but horribly bent, with all the leaves blown flat against the branches before a tremendous, silent gale.

But though the backdrop was depressing, the people weren't. Their economic situation generally was bad, of course, but the average person seemed not nearly so wretched as those who had gone downtown to seek out Fiorello for personal help. In fact, the people in that area gave the impression of throbbing life. They were active, determined not simply to survive but to go on loving life itself. Kids ran in droves. Tolerant, amiable, good-natured mothers looked on with the air of having completed self-evident, all-fulfilling missions in life. Pushcart transactions were at once traditional ceremonies and enjoyable battles of wits. There was plenty of color, too, and a surging movement on the sidewalks like endless combers on a sandy beach. It seemed to me that most of the people I saw were complete extroverts in comparison to the sufferers downtown—the engineers and architects on their cheerless, futile rounds, seeking non-existent employment and revealing in their drawn faces the extent of their inner damage. This was especially true of the young college graduates. With experts of standing out of work, they didn't have the ghost of a chance. They took terrible punishment. To this day, the distilled agony of the depression, to me, is symbolized by a spotlessly clean white collar, frayed to its very threads. Poverty, whether on Morningside Heights or in Harlem below it, is destructive, but the man from the Heights suffered a paralysis of soul that seemed unknown in Harlem. It may be that Morningsiders died inside attempting to conceal their troubles, while the Harlemites openly, unashamedly, and healthily pooled theirs.

Marc and I climbed into the back of a big delivery truck equipped with a movable loudspeaker and ordinary wooden benches along the sides. There were a couple of other people already there. Bunting festooned the outsides, and pictures of Fiorello with Republican eagles, and his own symbol, the Liberty Bell, at the four corners completed the *décor*. A small group cheered as we drove off. The truck jounced downtown a few blocks, where a very large crowd was awaiting us. Our truck went slowly through the crowd, turned into a sidestreet, and stopped. The tailgate was let down, and the microphone was moved to the very end of the truck. All was ready. The crowd eddied up to the very edge of the tailgate; the street was packed with people on all sides of us.

I sat on the bench, reviewing my notes, as things got under way. I remember the purplish arc lights, and the shadow of a wire in front of it swinging back and forth like a pendulum. I wasn't nearly as nervous as I thought I'd be.

Marc muttered over his shoulder that I was on next. Then I did feel a little queasy. Marc was doing the introducing. I got up and stood alongside him. I heard myself described as a distinguished young visitor who was thoroughly familiar with all of the grave national problems of the day and who enjoyed the confidence of our great leader, Fiorello H. La Guardia, short cheer, your mike. I grabbed it and started to talk.

It was generally agreed in newspaper circles that La Guardia and Bob La Follette had the most informed, socially conscious electorates in the country. It was an education to me, during that campaign, to see the concentrated attention which was bestowed on every speaker. There was no nonsense about the content of speeches. They could not be general: the sense of the meeting was that either you had something to say or you hadn't. The red carpet that might have been laid out for you could be snapped out from under your feet at any moment if you failed to live up to your billing.

I opened up on the City Trust, as I had planned. I had intended merely to outline it in general, but I found such rapport that I was able to go into it in detail. From the record, I named the names and charged the crimes. The Democratic leaders were heavily involved, and I cited chapter and verse. The obvious conclusion I hammered home: Who could be found to oppose the election of La Guardia, save those content to send a thief to office? "Thief" is as strong a word in Harlem as anywhere else. I was greatly satisfied with the reception I received, but I saw Marc looking at me narrowly.

Marc then took over the microphone, and there ensued what can only be described as a mass phenomenon. He started slowly and spoke for some time. Then abruptly he struck his heel on the truck bed; it made a loud hollow noise and the crowd stirred. The cadence of his talk increased, and soon the heel struck again. Again the pace quickened. I sensed rather than heard the reaction of his listeners. His voice rose, and now the heel struck more often with the beginnings of a real tempo. It began to sound like a train leaving a station. The crowd mirrored his growing excitement. At the climax, Marc was shouting at the top of his lungs and he was stamping his foot as hard and as rapidly as a flamenco dancer. The crowd pulsed to the rhythm and at last found release in a tumultuous, prolonged roar of applause. Because it was good theater, it was also great politics.

Later that evening, back at headquarters, some men came over and asked me if I didn't think the only way out of the transit problem was receivership for the city subways and eventual municipal ownership. I said I wasn't sure, that I hadn't looked that far into it. Another group asked me if I didn't think the Federal Reserve should make risky equity loans direct, as a pump primer; I said I did. There were a half-dozen questions which indicated that many of those present were at least as familiar with government finance as most Congressmen, and certainly more knowledgeable than I.

When I saw Fiorello the next day, I could tell he was not pleased. "Ernest," he asked, almost plaintively, "what the hell did you do up there last night?" He pushed his glasses up on his forehead.

"Nothing," I said. "I just attacked the City Trust banditry, that's all."

Fiorello sighed. "Now They will be pouring money in there to beat me." He looked both gloomy and nettled.

"Who?" I asked in amazement. "Who'll pour in money against you because of *my* speech?"

"Why, Wall Street, the Big Banks." He made a sweeping gesture. "They were fighting me generally, but now it's personal. The Big Banks have done the same damn' things as the City Trust, and now you've gone and frightened them at just the wrong time. Money will *pour* in against me. Well, it can't be helped now."

I just couldn't picture the Boards of Directors of the big banks downtown scurrying into executive session because of an obscure speech by a law clerk on a street corner in Harlem. I said as much. Fiorello shook his head. "No," he said, "the Democratic leaders are probably downtown right now, collecting thousands." I had mad visions of fleets of armored cars rushing gold bullion uptown posthaste, with Morgan and Aldrich wringing their hands and praying it was enough. It was, I thought, too silly for words. Yet the idea was enormously flattering. I felt like a young Disraeli, regretful that his first speech had upset the balance of power in Europe but determined to be resolute about it all. "Well," I soothed, "let's wait and see."

Presumably the Money Barons refused to be stampeded into parting with their cash, because nothing was ever heard of it again. I decided, however, to concentrate thereafter on Fiorello's voting record and his Congressional leadership. There was material enough there, Heaven knew, because Fiorello had taken a position on practically every bill before Congress during his tenure of office.

The speakers were eventually assigned to specific trucks, and the trucks made specific stops. Most of the speaking took place between 8:00 and 10:30 P.M. Fiorello himself would often speak at the final gathering of the evening, and he drew immense crowds. He was eloquent, factual, and sincere; he always ended on a fighting note, and he had them with him all the way. Our "enemies" deliberately scheduled a meeting one night for the same time and place as a meeting we had announced, at which Fiorello was slated to speak. Fiorello got there early and climbed up on the truck with us. A large crowd of La Guardia supporters was on hand. Sure enough, as the appointed hour drew near, a huge mob of people accompanied by a band could be heard coming up the avenue. Our opponents stopped about a block from the edge of our crowd. Between the two groups stood one lone policeman. Suddenly both crowds became absolutely silent. They faced each other like two shaggy, unfriendly animals.

"Ernest," said Fiorello, very quietly, "go and tell that cop we were here first and we're staying. Tell him," he said, "that if the Law can't protect us, we can protect ourselves." I rose to go, but he caught me by the sleeve and added: "Get tough with him. And if you have to hit him, don't hesitate."

My stomach muscles froze. "You mean *hit* the *cop?*" I bleated unbelievingly.

"Yes," said Fiorello. "Punch him in the eye if he tries to finagle us."

There is an old superstition among newsmen that it is very bad luck indeed to sock a New York cop, and I had seen strong evidence, as an ex-reporter myself, in support of it. But down I clambered from the truck and made my way through the crowd; or rather, a way opened for me. I passed the outer fringe of our followers with all the enthusiasm of a space cadet leaving the earth's gravitational field in a faulty rocket. I advanced on the cop, thinking we two were like Sohrab and Rustum meeting between the opposing lines. Just before I reached him, I looked back at Fiorello under the arc light, and he nodded his head vigorously by way of reassurance. I straightened my shoulders, walked the rest of the way, and aggressively stuck out my jaw.

"Listen," I snarled. "La Guardia says we were here first and we're gonna stay here. If you can't enforce the law, we'll do it for you."

He was a bulky young Irishman, about my age. He poked his face right into mine.

"*You* listen," he said. "I got eyes. Tell him to keep his shirt on. And I don't need no help from nobody." He turned on his heel, faced the other crowd, and, moving his arms as if he were shooing chickens, he started walking toward them. "Beat it," he said to them. "Go on, beat it." They hesitated for a moment, then broke. A couple of blocks away, their band struck up and they all marched off. I was dizzy with relief. There was no question about it: Fiorello would have resorted to violence then and there had it been necessary.

That select corps of La Guardia zealots, the Ghiboneys, usually convoyed the trucks in groups of three or four in case we were molested. Often, we were. One night Marc and I noticed that little knots of people were forming

within the crowd; something had happened. Suddenly
Marc said, "They're dropping bricks from the roof!"
There was a great swirl. Our men, presumably Ghiboneys,
dashed into the nearest tenement and ran up to the roof.
We could hear them shouting back and forth as they made
their way through the forest of chimneys, hunting for the
miscreants. At that point a scuffle started near the tailgate.
Suddenly Marc launched right out into the air and landed
on top of a milling group. These tactics appalled me because (*a*) you can't lick a bunch by mixing with it, (*b*) if
you ever go under you'll never get up, (*c*) Marc wasn't
built for street fighting, and (*d*) if you're ever going to get
a knife in the ribs, this is where. But obviously I couldn't
just stand there, so I took a deep breath and leaped after
him, roughly shoving people aside until I got to him. He
was flailing away at a great rate.

"Get going!" I yelled. "Get going!" and I shoved a few
smaller types back. A vague circle cleared around us. Marc
gave everybody a verbal lashing, and like two ruffled ban-
tam roosters we climbed back on the truck. To this day, I
don't know what Marc thought he was breaking up, or who
he thought he was assisting.

A woman had been hit by a falling brick. (The Ghiboneys failed to flush their quarry.) Fiorello took the news
of the injured woman very gravely. Someone had got her
name and address, and he told me to go over and see how
she was. It was about eleven-thirty when I arrived at the
address, a very dingy tenement. There were three or four
men standing by the door, and they silently barred the way
when I asked about her. You could have cut their suspicion
with a knife. I said that Congressman La Guardia had sent

me, and that he was very concerned. One man spoke. He said no one was injured; everything was all right. I got the feeling that they were relatives of hers, and that they were standing guard over her. Could I see her, I asked. Everything was all right, the man insisted. Could Congressman La Guardia do anything to help? No one was injured; everything was all right. I thanked them. They acknowledged my thanks with brief nods. I left. Fiorello seemed to understand it all better than I did. "They've learned to be cautious," he said. "It's a sad comment."

At another time I was talking at the mike on a dark, cavernous side street when someone threw a baby carriage off the roof. It missed me, landing on the cab of the truck like a clap of thunder. Glass smashed, and a roar went up from the crowd, but no one was hurt. I had jumped several feet into the air, hanging on to the microphone, and as I landed I shouted into it with masterful irrelevancy, "I can lick any bastard in the crowd!" The melee soon subsided, the Ghiboneys again swarmed up to the roof, but again no one was found. It was widely agreed that I had made a great fool of myself, and the story stuck to me. As recently as last year I met one of Fiorello's friends at a dinner party who laughed till the tears came as he described the scene. The table was enchanted; I smiled feebly.

We were told one day that a great Washington newspaperman was coming up to speak for Fiorello. Fiorello himself acted faintly impressed. This big gun was to go out on a truck with us, and Fiorello would join us all for the finale of the evening. When the Monarch of the Press arrived, it was apparent that the royal progress had been made through lakes of bathtub gin. He fairly reeked of it, and it had induced an amiable, foolish grin. A man of foresight, he carried a large reserve bottle in his overcoat pocket. He squinted at the headquarters scene with warm approval, which he voiced in genial, if thick tones. We finally got him hoisted aboard the truck, and off we went.

The crowds were expecting the celebrity. In a way, they were warmed-up audiences, anxious to applaud anyone who had come all the way from Washington to pay tribute to Fiorello. In his first address the columnist rumbled amiably along, and the eager listeners rendered appropriate applause during his frequent pauses. Finally, he pulled himself more or less together and shouted hoarsely that he hadn't really come all this distance to support a politician; he had made the journey to support a man who fought "for your kid and mine." The response was thunderous; kids were very popular in Harlem. The outburst visibly startled the befuddled speaker, and it was apparent he was working hard on a clinching sentence. He simply switched to the plural. He spread his arms wide and bellowed, "Yes, for my kids and yours!" He bowed his head as the benediction of applause rolled over him in waves. He sat down happily on the wooden bench and we lurched away. He stared straight in front of him and took a thoughtful swig. I wondered how many children he had, if any.

He kept swigging away as the evening progressed. We thought we'd better put him on to speak first at the remaining stops, and cut our own talks short, because no one knew what might happen. Before long he was concluding every paragraph with the "my kids and yours" bit. And, I'll admit, with great effect. We all kept our talks to a minimum and told the driver to speed it up between stops. We fairly flew along on our appointed rounds. The guy was absolutely sensational at all of them.

Naturally, we were at the final meeting place very early, and I asked him if he didn't want to rest. I made a pillow of my topcoat, and he stretched out on the floor of the truck, stared straight up into the sky, and sang to himself until we saw Fiorello arriving and got him up. Fiorello asked him how he felt, and he said he felt fine. He delivered his speech again, and this time he and the kids got the biggest ovation of all. At the conclusion of the evening, we swung him off the truck with a wild thrashing of arms and legs, like a giraffe in a cargo sling. Three or four of his friends had come up to get him, and with the greatest fuss imaginable they got him into a cab. He waved merrily from the back seat, hanging halfway out the window, a tipsy monarch bidding farewell to a carnival crowd of colorful peasants. He was in a marvelous mood. He was a smash hit, and he knew it.

An elderly lady came into the office one afternoon, apparently a shopkeeper of small means. She was on a mysterious errand; she said she wanted to give the money, *this time*, to Mr. La Guardia himself. "*This* time?" frowned Fiorello, "Show her in."

She explained to him that one of our ward leaders had asked her for twenty-five dollars for a secret La Guardia campaign fund, and she had given him fifteen dollars. The balance, she had made up her mind, she would hand to Fiorello himself, to be sure he got it. Fiorello called in one of the girls, and the woman told her story while it was taken down. La Guardia explained to her that he wanted to keep our records straight. It was immediately typed up, and La Guardia read it to her. He told her if what she had said was true, he would like her to sign it. She signed. Then Fiorello phoned the Police Commissioner and asked him to investigate. The Commissioner apparently asked why, because Fiorello barked, "Because there's a chance one of *my* leaders may be a crook!" That, I thought, took real political guts.

Toward the end of the campaign I was having an early dinner down at the Little Venice with some friends one night when the headwaiter came over with a message: Mr. La Guardia wanted me uptown right away. I said to tell him I'd be along as soon as I finished eating. The captain came back and said it was urgent, that I was to leave immediately. With the air of a Foreign Secretary being called away from his house guests by a fussy Prime Minister, I excused myself. The deferential captain hurried me into my coat. I felt like Sheridan hurrying up to Winchester. The spirit of the Alamo and the Relief of Lucknow pervaded me. To the Rescue! I arrived at headquarters, and half a dozen people said in hushed voices, "The Major wants you." It was like walking through a verbal arch of crossed swords: "The Major wants you."

The Major greeted me with a hearty "Ah!" as if my arrival meant he could stop worrying. He quickly motioned me into a huddle. I knew I was the envy of all.

"Ernest," he whispered, "they're going to pull the fire alarm when I speak tonight." He drew back as if aghast at the terrible secret he had just imparted to me, and his expression suggested that I too must be confounded by such a diabolical plot. I couldn't imagine what this had to do with me and my mad dash uptown. I had expected that Fiorello was at least going to seek a temporary injunction against the United States Navy, or some such outlandish dramatic move that would rock the nation back on its heels.

"Why," I said absently, "they'll never get away with it."

This was greeted with vociferous enthusiasm by Fiorello. He clapped me heartily on the back. "Attaboy!" he said. "Get right over there."

"Get over where?" I asked, completely bewildered.

"Over to the fire alarm box," he said, "and punch anybody in the eye who comes near it!"

My Foreign Secretarial robes slid from my shoulders to the floor in an untidy heap. Visions of the Alamo and Lucknow dimmed. I wasn't even a bodyguard, I reflected; I was a bouncer. "Wait a minute," I said. "Suppose there *is* a fire? *Then* what do I do?"

"There won't be any," he assured me impatiently. "There hasn't been one in that vicinity for fifty years. Hurry up, now. Get going!"

I made my way outside, running a gauntlet of eager questions, but I just held up one hand and shook my head: Atlas staggering under the secret burden of the world. But to myself I thought bitterly, Big Deal for a Big Shot. I perspired with humiliation: if anybody were to find out the real reason why I had been called, I'd never live it down.

I took up my lonely vigil by the fire alarm box, feeling definitely subhuman. To make matters worse, one of those cold autumn rains began to fall with a quiet, discouraging persistence.

About nine-thirty a cab drew up in the drizzle. The door flew open and a cheerful voice called out: "Hey, Mr. President! Come on, get in. He's not speaking tonight after all."

It was Mimi, in fine spirits, naturally, over my discomfiture. With cheerful malice, he said, "Never mind; 'they also serve who only stand and wait.'"

I always felt a little guilty about the superlative service I received thereafter at the Little Venice, but I never disillusioned them about my errand.

Fiorello was a dynamo throughout the campaign—absolutely tireless. People waited to see him in long lines, and he saw every one of them. He kept tabs on the smallest detail, but could switch from a trivial registry question to a fiery speech concerning basic issues on no notice at all. He was everywhere at once, encouraging, strengthening, and inspiring us all.

In the last days before the election he told me that I was to function as a Deputy Attorney General of New York. Each side was allowed a few to patrol the Election. I went downtown and was sworn in. The night before election I will never forget. Fiorello sent for me and we went off by ourselves behind a big screen. His powerful jaw was set. He said, "Ernest, what are you going to do if they try to steal the election tomorrow?" His eyes glittered with a thousand lights, like the hard, cold glitter in the eyes of a poised black panther. I was almost hypnotized; I know I had difficulty swallowing before I could speak.

"Listen, Major," I said. "I took an oath and I'll live up to it. I know a crime when I see one. Nobody has to tell me what to do!"

"What will you do?" he persisted.

"I'll arrest them," I said angrily, "or get killed trying to."

He put his hand on my arm. "No," he said, "we don't

want arrests; we want votes. If they rush the machine, knock them away from it. Then cast as many votes for me as they stole. You hear? Vote until they knock you out! Tomorrow," he continued, "I've given you a post of honor. Ernest, it's dangerous." I was about to deprecate this when he said slowly: "They might shoot you. You could be killed."

Well, that's just dandy, I thought; from baby carriages on the bean to bullets in the chest. "For God's sake, then, give me a gun!"

"No," Fiorello said deliberately, "you can't have a gun. I'd sooner see you dead than tried for murder."

"Well, *I* wouldn't," I assured him. "I want a gun."

"No," he said firmly and soothingly, as to a child, "you can't have a gun. And," he added sharply, "I don't want you to get one anywhere else. You hear? If you don't want to go, you don't have to, but you can't take a gun. Understand?" He must have been reading my mind; I had been thinking, Why ask him? Somewhere I'd get a pistol that night. Now that was out. I promised I wouldn't get a gun, and we parted.

But I got sorer and sorer the more I thought about it. I tried to catch his eye, but he evaded me. I went over later in the evening and tapped him on the shoulder. "No gun," he said levelly, without even looking at me, and went right on talking to the person he was with.

Fiorello's climactic speech that night was unforgettable. The finale of every La Guardia campaign was a great ceremony. It always took place at his Lucky Corner, 116th and Lexington. Thousands of people were on hand, a moving demonstration of faith by people who regarded

Fiorello not only as their own champion, but as the champion of humanity as a whole. There was almost a religious fervor about it. Fiorello spoke, and his soul was in every word. Never had his integrity, all his gifts, found better expression. He was a charging lion. As he concluded, a searchlight played down on him from somewhere above. And at the end the tumult of the crowd was such as must have toppled the Walls of Jericho.

I slept very little that night. I just lay in bed and stared at the ceiling of my darkened room. It was unthinkable that Fiorello would send me into a gun fight without a gun. I tried to believe it was just like the night before a big game, but that wasn't true. Noel Coward once described his sensations before an opening—as though his stomach were a paper bag with a sparrow fluttering inside. But my stomach seemed to have shriveled to a hard, wrinkled walnut. Dawn came at last and I got ready to go uptown. The polls opened at 6:00 A.M. I ate no breakfast because I had read somewhere that if you were shot the difference between life and death could be the presence of food in your stomach. The theory was that the food poisoned the wound. I didn't believe it, but I was taking no chances.

I arrived at my assigned location at 5:45. There was already a short line of voters outside. I noticed a little boy playing with a hoop by the door, and I thought it was a hell of an hour for a kid to be up. The polling place was a long store with windows on both sides of the entrance. The registration books were to the right as you entered, and the voting booths were further back and on the left, over against the wall. Near the window to the right of the door stood three young seminary students, representing the

Honest Ballot League, as I recall. The inspectors were already seated. Two policemen in bull harness were at their stations near the curtained voting booths.

So was our opponent's man, a little older than I, and about my size. I took off my topcoat and hung it up.

The voting started. The first voter came in, checked with the inspectors, and entered the booth. The opposition man brazenly moved the curtain aside with his hand and peered in. I challenged the vote at once and told the cops to make an arrest. They suggested that I just take it easy. The Tammany man walked out with the voter. I followed. I told the three young clerics to stand by, there was going to be trouble. I went outside and discovered my adversary passing down the line, openly handing out money from a large roll of bills.

By this time the second voter had completed inspector's check and was going into the booth. Back came the Tammany man and again he poked his head inside the curtain. And again I challenged the vote, with same negative results.

A third man came in, checked, stepped into the booth. As the Tammany man raised the curtain to watch the vote, I belted him on the jaw with everything I had. He went flying into the machine and collapsed to the floor. All hell broke loose. The two cops jumped me, and I locked with one of them. We scuffled and cuffed, and the cop yelled that I was under arrest. I said *he* was. Neither cop, I noticed, went for his gun; in fact, the other cop was now engaged in picking up the fallen man. With the heightened perception one tends to have in moments of crisis, I saw that the young clerics were praying and that the little boy outside was jumping excitedly up and down and waving his hat.

The cop and I had just broken apart, still arresting each other, when a huge limousine hurtled to a screaming stop at the curb. Men tumbled out of it and came running into the store. This is it, I thought. I just stood there, waiting for the bullets. I felt naked, and my arms were going up and down in short jerks like a pawing bear. "Now and at the hour of our death, Amen," came fleetingly to mind from out of my childhood. It was all over in seconds. In all, seven men rushed in, their right hands in their pockets. *But* they wore great big La Guardia buttons in their lapels! They formed a semicircle around me, facing the cops, and just stood there, crouched. Not a word. I regained my voice, and from behind my barrier I told the cop again that those first three votes were challenged. He said he'd heard me the first time. The fellow I had hit was on his feet now, and the second cop was helping him wash his face at a sink at the back of the store.

Now another black car roared up and out jumped Fiorello. He apparently knew all about what had happened because he burst in shouting, "Attaboy, Ernest, give 'em hell!" He tongue lashed the cops and said they'd go to prison if there was any more nonsense. He said they'd date time for the rest of their lives from the second anything funny happened there again. I saw that the La Guardia men were leaving, and I asked one of them in a low voice where they were from.

He whispered: "Friends of Fiorello. Amalgamated Clothing Workers of America."

Fiorello looked around defiantly and then motioned for

me to leave with him. We got into the car. "There won't be any more trouble there," he said. Then, "Are you all right?" I started to say that of course I was all right, but instead I broke into a torrent of tears. I was as surprised as Fiorello. He said what was I crying for, I had done fine. For a moment or two I couldn't stop. I had seen football players cry in the dressing room after a tough game, and it isn't exactly crying so much as a release of tension, but I had never been affected that way before. Fiorello gazed out of the window while I pulled myself together, and for the rest of the ride he was gruffly kind.

He was right; there was no more trouble that day. The fellow I had hit was gone when I went back in the afternoon, but he soon reappeared. It was awkward at first, but it seemed to me that he was actually trying to be friendly. He smiled, and I went over and said I was sorry that I had had to belt him. He said to forget it, it was all part of the game. He stuck out his hand and I shook it.

Fiorello carried that particular precinct by less than fifty votes. But it was obvious that over-all it was a Democratic landslide from Buffalo to the Battery. By eleven, we knew the bad news. Fiorello had lost a very close race.

I felt terrible. We walked up the dark street together. At the corner he stopped. "Well, Ernest," he said, "we did our damnedest. And you can't do better than that. Now go home and get some rest." I told him I didn't want to, but he ordered me to go. I didn't know what to do. I wanted desperately to help him. I went on down the block alone and crossed the street. Then I looked back. He was talking to some people who had come along. They parted and he walked on by himself. I followed him, keeping well back on the opposite side of the street, hoping something would occur to me to do, but nothing did. He climbed the steps to his house and walked in, closing the door gently behind him. I never felt so miserable in my life as I did standing there on that street. I don't know how long it was before I turned and started the long walk home.

XIII

Within a month after his defeat, Fiorello was busy regaining lost ground. Postcard invitations were sent to a special list of people known to be actively interested in better government for New York City, and a meeting was held in Town Hall. An audience of over five hundred showed up and warmly applauded Fiorello's calm, cool speech. In the main they were old faithfuls—the hard nucleus of Fiorello's support. As had happened in the past, Fiorello was down to base strength, laying careful foundations for a new edifice to be built on the ruins of an old defeat.

However careful or logical his plans may have been, his immediate future was to be shaped by a seemingly unrelated series of events which he could not possibly have anticipated. This chancy chain of events began four years before with a gambling game and a pistol shot. It is not too extravagant to borrow a page from history by saying that this was a shot heard eventually round the world, for it had a direct bearing on the subsequent election of two men to the highest elective offices in the land. The figurative ricochet of this bullet radically changed the complexion of party politics in New York City and in Albany; and at least the echo of the explosion rang through the corridors of the White House.

The gentleman on the receiving end of the literal bullet was, of course, Arnold Rothstein, Banker to the Underworld, one of the most verminous characters that ever infested New York City. One October evening in 1928, two notorious big-shot gamblers, "Titanic" Thompson and "Nigger Nate" Raymond, anxious for some action, invited Arnold Rothstein to participate in a game of High Spade. The evening's diversion was expensive for Rothstein; he lost $340,000. He resolved this dilemma in characteristic fashion: he welshed. But this proved even more expensive. On a Saturday night early in November, he received, while dining at Lindy's, another cordial invitation, this time from gambler George McManus, to attend a floating crap game at the Park Central Hotel, a few blocks north. Rothstein bustled out, his sporting blood aroused. At 11:10 P.M. Mr. Rothstein was found at the service entrance of said hospice, his right side punctured by a .38 bullet, a wound of which he subsequently died at Polyclinic Hospital on the following Tuesday. On his deathbed Rothstein had only enough strength to caution his friends and well-wishers everywhere, including his lawyer, to keep their mouths shut; and, having completed his last furtive act, he died, thereby performing the one act of public service ever connected with his name.

In the meantime thirty-five New York City detectives were halfheartedly going through the motions of finding out who did the shooting. The murderer was never caught.

Up to the day of his timely demise, Rothstein had always made it a point to know the price of every corrupt official in the city, and always had the money to pay it. He knew to a penny the market on lost souls, from rigged security operators and horse race fixers down to what a Bowery bum would do for the glass of rotgut whisky that was killing him. And Rothstein traded on it all. If Rothstein alive had been an unsavory article, Rothstein dead was a calamity. His activities had not been limited to the dregs of society; on the contrary, certain of his dealings had involved some very eminent citizens indeed. The publication of his records might make for embarrassment, it was felt. Not to put too fine a point on it, City Hall was in an uproar. Mayor Walker was unhappy and upset.

After the killing the police went to Rothstein's fortress home and seized his voluminous files. A judge ordered that they be put in the custody of a Tammany district leader—for "safekeeping." Although it took two trucks to move them, the trustee shortly reported to the Court that they had been stolen, and the Court solemnly accepted this explanation.

But at least one record actually was missing, for in 1929, when he went down to crushing defeat in the mayoralty race against Jimmy Walker, Fiorello produced it. It was the record of a loan of $19,940 from Rothstein to a pitiful excuse of a magistrate named Albert Vitale, of the Bronx. That was the touch-off match to the powder train which was to blow the old Tammany Hall to smithereens forever.

There were two Democrats in New York State who bore no more love for Tammany than Fiorello did. One was the distinguished Judge Samuel Seabury, who had been done out of the Governorship by the Wigwam in 1916; the other was Franklin D. Roosevelt, whose first act in public life fifteen years before had been to stamp on Tammany's toes for opposing his election as State Senator. The paths of Fiorello, Seabury, and Roosevelt were to converge with effects important to the nation's history. The man who brought them together was Adolf A. Berle, Jr., Professor of Corporate Finance at Columbia University. In 1928, however, no one of the men involved had any more notion that this would occur than Arnold Rothstein himself, laid out in Brooklyn in his pine box, for once in a game he couldn't fix.

The Appellate Division named Judge Seabury to investigate the Magistrates' Courts. It was open knowledge at the time that magistrates' appointments were sold to loyal and zealous ward heelers. Some of the magistrates really represented a family enterprise. All relatives who had two dimes to rub together went into the pool, the family had the honor of including a judge in their number, and everyone sat back for dividends. The caliber of this Bench can be imagined, but not described.

Seabury went after his quarry cautiously, even though he had the backing of the press. It is a phenomenon of all investigations that the "breaks" come in the form of volunteer witnesses once the investigations are announced. The Magistrates' Courts investigation went true to form. One night there walked into the New York *Daily News* office a desperately ill little pimp by the name of Chile Acuna. Lowell Limpus interviewed him. Acuna said he was tired of framing innocent women for the Vice Squad and helping to railroad them before crooked magistrates. A pimp is not the world's most reliable witness, and the *News* checked carefully. What they found disgusted a city which was used to stenches: one woman magistrate had actually doctored the court records in her zeal to protect the police-vice ring. Innocent women had been framed, all right, and by the dozen.

This set off a second investigation: the Hofstadter Committee to investigate corruption in New York City, with, again, the implacable Sam Seabury as its counsel.

Mayor Walker tried to wisecrack it out of existence. He paraded across the line of fire with leers and knowing winks to vociferous if cynical applause; but when he was in complete command of his faculties—which was seldom in those later days—the strain made his skin look like old parchment. From Washington, Fiorello threw what assistance he could to Seabury; but there was a game of far larger stakes developing, and no one knew it more than the agile incumbent at Albany, Governor Franklin D. Roosevelt.

Roosevelt certainly loved Tammany no better than did La Guardia or Seabury, but, unlike them, he needed the Hall badly. He was an all-out candidate for the Presidency and, if he got it, a hands-down choice to win. Now Roosevelt was in a dilemma. Every bit of the shocking evidence Seabury was unearthing made headlines across the nation. Tammany, an absolute necessity to Roosevelt until his nomination, would be a millstone around his neck west of the Hudson once he had it. With his usual perfect timing, however, F.D.R. pulled the neatest political trick of the year, and it landed him squarely in the center ring of the Big Top for two performances and a double encore.

Meanwhile, Seabury had assembled a highly competent staff of accountants and lawyers and told them to see what they could find. To no one's surprise, they found plenty. The various machine leaders had large amounts of money, the explanation of which convulsed the nation with hoots of angry laughter. Wonderful Damon Runyonesque characters were uncovered: Tin Box Farley (no relation to James, of course) whose only explanation for his funds was that he had simply found them in his little tin box; the fifty-four starving McQuades who were the ridiculous excuse offered by that rascal for his bulging deposit box; and mighty Jimmy Hines, caught far up the creek, not only without a paddle, but in the same boat with the master gangster Dutch Schultz. The Board of Standards and Appeals, which had jurisdiction of zoning and building permits, was exposed as a million-dollar-a-year racket, but only after Tammany had challenged Seabury's subpoena up to the Court of Appeals and lost.

The contest had all the drama and violence of a heavyweight championship fight. Crafty old Judge Seabury kept boring in with heavy body punches, and the Democratic Party winced as far north as Albany when his crashing right landed on its soft underbelly, Tammany. There was no doubt as to what Seabury's knockout blow was to be. He had, in the parlance of the fight game, telegraphed his punch: it was going to be a crushing overhand right, tagged for the political glass jaw of one James J. Walker.

The Seabury technique was coldly methodical. It took time, but under the paralyzing body blows of exposure after exposure Tammany was at last brought to bay, breathing heavily and badly hurt. The trail of blood left by the dying Rothstein led straight to the paths of corruption within the city machine, and those paths were narrowing rapidly in the direction of the back door of the Wigwam. All at once it was too late for Jimmy's fancy footwork; he was going down for the full count unless saved by the referee—i.e., Governor Roosevelt.

In desperation, Tammany went into a clinch. It hung on with the claim of constitutional privilege and the rule applying to burden of proof in a criminal case. Seabury had proved big, unexplained, and inexplicable bank accounts, but he still had to prove, and beyond a reasonable doubt, that these sums actually represented graft in order to make a case.

As 1932 rolled in, Governor Roosevelt viewed the untidy New York scene with absolutely unmixed emotions: everyone knew he was out for himself. He preferred to remain 150 miles north, in Albany, away from the furious scuffle in progress, and thus avoid the consequences of any wild swings. For Seabury's sake he deplored, and for Tammany's he demurred, an elegant exhibition on the high-wire if there ever was one.

But ringwise Sam Seabury knew that F.D.R. was in a tough spot, and he decided to capitalize on it. He suddenly declared that he was not conducting a criminal trial, but a legislative inquiry, thereby taking off his back the heavy burden of proof. He stated that the proof he had was not intended for a Grand Jury action: it was meant for Governor Roosevelt, and he laid it at Roosevelt's feet, thereby making himself the most unwelcome visitor in the Upper Hudson Valley since Gentleman Johnny Burgoyne.

The nation held its breath; it looked as if the New York Governor was cornered. A rapid look at the spring calendar —instead of the issues—quickly decided the man on the

high wire. F.D.R. simply had to have Tammany support
for the convention, still three months away. To the amazement of all, and the admiration of many, he resoundingly
denounced graft and corruption in general, but ruled that
Seabury had failed to make a case in particular. Tammany
breathed a sigh of relief heard across the nation. With this
heartening demonstration of party regularity in the face
of tremendous pressure, the big city machines of Jersey
City, Chicago, Kansas City, and New Orleans took a more
kindly view of the Squire of Hyde Park. Which only goes
to prove how little politicians know about politics. Jim
Farley took planes, trains, and busses to the far hinter-
lands and ultimately piloted F.D.R. through to the nomination for the Presidency at Chicago. With that accomplished
F.D.R. lost no time in letting it be known that the Tammany
millstone around his neck would shortly find itself at the
bottom of the sea. Everybody understood this but the Wigwam, which, in its innocence, was apparently unable to
comprehend such a fast double play.

Immediately after the Convention, Seabury examined
Walker, and then renewed his attack at Albany. In brief,
Seabury stated that there were large, unexplained amounts
of money in the hands of public officials, and that he
wanted another ruling from the Governor: though not
enough to convict, were they not enough to remove?
Fiorello also pressed the point. He sent me chasing for statements by Presidents Grover Cleveland and Theodore Roosevelt and, backed by them, he submitted that a public
office was a public trust, and what did Governor Roosevelt
intend to do about it all? F.D.R., the marvel of the high
wire, was waiting for just this cue. With a great flip, he

described a complete arc and a full about-face, declared that public office was *indeed* the highest of trusts, and descended gracefully to his waiting Admiral's cape as Commander-in-Chief, which he never thereafter doffed. His feat left Tammany holding the bag, in fact a lot of little black ones, which contained one-way tickets to Sing Sing. Only Roosevelt could have managed the stunt, and it was a question as to which he had more of—skill or brass.

Fiorello and I were at the intersection of Seventh Avenue and 47th Street when the newstrucks came tearing into Times Square and the newsboys started shouting "Extra!" I ran over and got a paper with the headline "Roosevelt Sustains Seabury," and the subhead "Rules Public Officials Must Explain Private Funds." Fiorello scanned it and said very solemnly, "Ernest, this is a great day for our country."

Before the ink was dry on the extra, Jimmy Walker's sponge came sailing into the ring in the form of a one-sentence letter to the City Clerk: "I hereby resign as Mayor of New York City, James J. Walker." The Walker-La Guardia political duel was ended.

As the Lame Duck Congress opened, the President-elect declined interregnum cooperation with President-reject Hoover. F.D.R. had his own financial plans, a large part of which had been blueprinted by Adolf Berle, Jr. Berle, though he had known Fiorello only a few months, made the somewhat daring decision of making Fiorello F.D.R.'s spokesman in the last days of the dying Congress. Oddly enough, Fiorello became the savior of the railroads he so ardently disliked by jamming through the Railroad Bankruptcy and Reorganization bill. Far closer to his heart was the Farm and Home Mortgage Relief bill. And together Fiorello and Berle patterned the legislation that resulted in the famed "77B" of the Federal Bankruptcy Act, providing for an extension of private credit obligations under supervision of the Court. Altogether, it was perhaps the most active Lame Duck session in the nation's history. As the time came for Fiorello to step down and for F.D.R. to step up, the two men knew they had much in common, including one trustworthy friend in Berle.

During this period Judge Seabury kept slugging away. His revelations were such that the new Democratic Governor of New York, Herbert Lehman, a man of absolute personal honor, decided to appoint a Special District Attorney for New York County. The Seabury exposures had made corruption not a party issue, but a public cause. Governor Lehman, as a mark of his integrity, picked a man of the opposite party to root out and prosecute all civic irregularity. He was as honest as he was cold. Thomas E. Dewey was to go on to Albany three times as Governor, and he stopped twice at the very threshold of the White House. These things aside, he would still be remembered as the man who broke the hold of the Lepke, Luciano and Dutch Schultz gangs.

Fiorello was out and F.D.R. was in as the jockeying for the New York mayoralty race began in the spring of 1933. Early in May, Fiorello urged an anti-Tammany ticket to be headed by Al Smith, with Socialist Norman Thomas for Aldermanic President and Bob Moses for Comptroller. These nominations were duly made, with the fullest knowledge on Fiorello's part that none of the men named could possibly accept them. Fiorello, however, indicated that he stood ready to save the situation; if Al Smith wouldn't head the ticket, he, Fiorello, would.

A number of independent groups started a "Stop La Guardia" movement, working toward a joint ticket with the Republicans. It didn't look too good for Fiorello as the climax approached in late July. But Berle had arranged a series of private conferences between Seabury and Fiorello, as a result of which Seabury agreed to cast for Fiorello. When the showdown occurred early in August at the City Club, Berle and Seabury carried all before them. Fiorello came out of it with the Republican and Fusion nominations. It looked to be another rough, tough battle.

Fiorello adopted as his campaign song "Who's Afraid of the Big Bad Wolf," and the interminable tootling in the streets had people ready to start screaming. Overnight, however, it became "The Battle Hymn of the Republic," and the most fervid crusade in New York City's history was under way. The final lines seemed drawn.

But they weren't. The new man in the White House had a few ideas of his own. Without a word of warning, F.D.R. had Boss Ed Flynn of the Bronx split the Democratic ticket by nominating Joe McKee on a Recovery platform against the bumbling Tammany candidate, John O'Brien. At the same time, F.D.R. sent Berle to Cooper Union with a public White House repudiation of McKee! Roosevelt nominated McKee through Flynn and then denied him support through Berle—thus splitting the Democratic ticket. To nominate and then repudiate while allowing the nomination to stand is one for the books. It was. The books at final audit read: La Guardia—858,000; McKee—604,000; O'Brien—586,000.

Fiorello entered City Hall straight down the middle of F.D.R.'s split ticket. It was one of the nattiest double plays on file. Up in the Bronx and down on Fourteenth Street they still call it a double cross. Though the debate raged as to whether the President had pitched a ball or a strike, all were agreed that Fiorello was very nimble on the bases. Well, you have to be to steal home.

In Judge Samuel Seabury's home at exactly midnight on January 1, 1934, Fiorello H. La Guardia took the oath of office, administered by Supreme Court Justice Philip J. Mc-Cook, as Mayor of New York City. At exactly one minute after midnight, he ordered the arrest of the most notorious gangster in town—Lucky Luciano. His takeoff next morning was jet-propelled, and the momentum never let up until he stepped out of office twelve years later. He would dictate to secretaries in relays for at least twelve hours every day. No longer a legislator who had to persuade and negotiate, he now had what amounted to virtual dictatorship within his domain, and he pushed his prerogatives to the limit. When his labors ended, he had greatly altered the face of the city, from its charter to its highways, from its hospitals to its high schools. The outpouring of his prodigious energies was strictly in line with the convictions he had always held. He set about realizing his theories at boiler-works tempo.

At the end of his first six months, he rendered a report to the people. Among other things, 400 new playgrounds had been opened in that period and the city had begun to distribute milk, at cost, to the poorer sections. The hospital system was completely revised; so was the setup of the Health Department. All sorts of food-market racketeers were on the run. Almost every Department had felt his none too gentle hand, and had heard during surprise visits harsh demands for greater economy and efficiency. Remarkably, though, considering all these new departures, he had wiped out the budget deficits; and the City Bonds, which were at 78 when he took office, were now over par. The bankers had enough confidence in him to give him an interest rate of 3/4 of 1 per cent, whereas historically Tammany had had to pay 4 per cent. Adolf Berle deserves much of the credit for this. One of Fiorello's first official acts was to appoint Berle City Chamberlain, with instructions to put the city's financial house in order.

Fiorello's fiscal policies were a pride and a joy to him. Public Utilities found themselves the recipient of a brand-new tax, and had their old ones lifted. Since, under the law, they are entitled to a fair return, however, it was also something of a consumers' sales tax for all the fanfare. But it paid off, and along with the cutting of non-performing officeholders, the city treasury soon began to show color in its cheeks—or, if you prefer, its checks. New Deal money flowed into the city. Berle continued on as a White House financial adviser, and the two Chief Almoners, Ickes and Hopkins, were old friends of Fiorello's. It was a source of immeasurable relief in the Capital to be able to make large grants, knowing that under Fiorello's gimlet eye every dime would go for its designated purpose. Federal Aid, of course, did a lot to lift the strain on the local treasury, but there was no doubt, in any event, that the city's credit was sound.

When the time came for Fiorello to refund some long-time obligations, he thought it would be a novel idea to

get the money from the R.F.C. The R.F.C. politely declined. The banks thereupon upped their interest rate to
4½ per cent. Fiorello at once threatened to go around the
country selling his own bonds in key cities. It never came
to that, however, because a compromise was finally reached.
During the hassle one of Fiorello's young socialite secretaries sought to act as mediator. He remarked that he
thought he could smooth the whole thing out: by a strange
coincidence he was spending the week end with the opposition's leading investment banker. "Don't apologize,"
snapped Fiorello. "A lot of young men aren't particular
where they sleep around on week ends!"

From the first, Fiorello, like a latter-day Al Raschid,
dropped in on municipal lodginghouses unannounced, taking his place in the lines, to see how the luckless were being treated. With the plight of the city's unemployed up-
permost in his mind, he spent much time and thought in
preparing a request for a record-breaking relief budget.
Typically, he left as little to chance as possible.

He completed his careful preparations for the presentation of his relief budget and then rolled up his sleeves.
Anticipating the constitutional issue, he declared that all
lawyers were semicolon boys—that they had retarded civilization more than cancer and smallpox combined. He
had determined to press for an over-all of about three billion dollars. He called to the first public hearing the
Chairman of the Board of the largest bank in the city, in-
tending to bait him into some sort of "Let-'em-eat-cake" remark. Aggressively, he asked the banker how much money
he thought it would take to keep his fellow citizens from
starvation. The banker, tipped off as to Fiorello's three

billion estimate, calmly stated that it might run to six billions, and Fiorello's sails flapped feebly and hung slack. The expected opposition developed from the political quarter. As Fiorello started to read his findings, he was interrupted by an alderman who declared that relief money was already being misdirected. The alderman had documentary evidence, sworn affidavits, no less, proving that prostitutes were receiving relief money. He demanded that the practice be stopped, and that the budget be curtailed to the extent that these women were included. Fiorello bent upon the alderman his best busy-browed glare. "I thought that question was settled two thousand years ago, but I see I was wrong. Mr. Sergeant-at-Arms," he thundered, "clear the room! Clear the room—so this big bum can throw the first stone!"

As had been widely predicted, Fiorello's activities as Mayor were consistent with all his previous views. He continued to go down the line for Labor with a capital *L;* in any given dispute he did exactly what might have been expected of him, though theoretically his was now an impartial position. All of his craft, and he was a very crafty man indeed, was employed for the benefit of working people. With the power of City Hall behind it, his opinion very frequently was decisive. It all came under the head of ministerial prerogative, but the ruthlessness with which it was applied left no doubt as to his personal bias or the inevitable result of any given issue. At one point all the waiters in the city went out on strike. Their strike may or may not have been doing too well. At any rate, the city's hotels and larger restaurants managed to carry on—that is, until Fiorello entered the scene. What he did was classically simple: under the Health Law the city could inspect anyone handling food at any time. Fiorello, without warning, chose the height of the evening dinner hour to order a health inspection of all the scab waiters on duty, thus paralyzing service. The managements didn't like the findings either: several waiters were found to be suffering from contagious diseases. The inspections ceased as soon as an agreement with the regular waiters was reached, which was very shortly. The Building and Fire departments were preparing to make elaborate inspections when the managements came to terms.

At another time girl laundry workers went on strike. They were badly underpaid, and their working conditions were very poor. Hearkening back to the sweatshop era, and Fiorello's part in the fight against them, it was no surprise that as Mayor he would be their vigorous champion. Under the guise of keeping order, he practically blockaded the laundries with squads of police. The laundry owners went to City Hall to protest. Fiorello received them with elaborate courtesy and listened most patiently to their complaint. That alone should have put them on their guard, but it didn't. They told him that he was interfering in a labor dispute, and that the city was supposed to be neutral. Fiorello heartily agreed. The labor-union leader tried to say something, but Fiorello told him to shut up. Fiorello then turned to the spokesman of the laundry owners and asked him if he had an application to make. The spokesman swept himself firmly into the saddle of Fiorello's Trojan horse by repeating that his sole desire was to have the city remain neutral. Fiorello asked that this request be made in writing. The laundry owners hastily complied with a written request that the city withdraw all support from either side. As soon as it was handed to him, Fiorello announced that the application was granted, and that the city henceforth would be absolutely neutral. Thereupon he picked up the telephone, called the Water Department, and blandly ordered the Water Commissioner to turn off the water in all laundries, since the city was neutral in the fight. The laundry owners collapsed on the spot.

Fiorello ran true to form in his ideal of public service, too. He expected to be besieged by officeseekers, and, to a degree, he was. But he disposed of this problem at once. Immediately after his election, he addressed his entire campaign headquarters force. He said, in a very few sentences, that a Cause, not a man, had succeeded; and now he had been elected the Chief Magistrate of the city. "My first qualification for this great office," he declared, "is my monumental personal ingratitude!" There was disgruntlement, of course, and even a few heartbreaks, but Fiorello never swerved from his position: he got the best people he could for the jobs at hand, especially the top ones. Some of his highest appointments went to men outside the city, a new precedent which caused much wailing and gnashing of teeth. But Fiorello maintained that he hired a man on his abilities and not on the basis of where he slept at night. He felt the strain, however. He told Adolf Berle one evening that he'd like to be able to say "yes" to everything which was asked of him, but that he had taken an oath of office which he intended to honor. "The Devil," said Fiorello, "is easy to identify. He appears as your best friend when you're terribly tired and makes a very reasonable request which you know you shouldn't grant."

After he got settled in, Fiorello was practically his own Police Commissioner. As an ex-Commanding Officer, he knew that nothing goes down to the ranks faster than the disposition of the command tent. He used to say that any variation at the center made for terrific wobbles around the circumference. He also believed that the most sensitive department in the city was the Police, so there was little astonishment in his insistence of City Hall support for honest cops. Very early in his administration, a physician who was a casual personal acquaintance got a ticket for illegal parking. The doctor forcefully told the young patrolman that the ticket was inacceptable, whereupon the boy arrested him and brought him to the station house. The physician afterward went down to City Hall in person to report this grievous wrong. Fiorello called the station house and asked to speak to the young patrolman. The captain of the precinct, who by this time had heard all the details, came on instead and was all apologies. He explained to the Mayor that the arresting officer was a rookie cop who just hadn't known any better. Fiorello, of course, hit the ceiling. "He's a better cop than you are," he raged, "and I called him up to tell him I was sending him a box of cigars. He's the kind of cop I want—and you're not!" The rookie got his cigars, delivered significantly by the Mayor's car, and Fiorello very nearly broke his superior. This story ran through the department like wildfire.

General O'Ryan, the Police Commissioner, was a stickler for form, and he and the Mayor did not get on any too well. One bitter February day, when the city was in the grip of one of the worst cold waves on record, O'Ryan issued an order stating that policemen must wear their coats in summer. The Mayor at once issued countermanding orders. The freezing city roared with laughter at this battle over what uniform would be worn in sweltering July. Trivial though the incident was, it resulted in O'Ryan's eventual resignation, which had long been brewing. Fiorello was not displeased; and it was fitting that the situation had come to a head over a quarrel relating to the comfort and well-being of the rank-and-file, whom Fiorello was always to defend at the expense, if necessary, of his own top brass.

A story once went the rounds to the effect that Police Commissioner Valentine, O'Ryan's successor, had put a bodyguard on Fiorello without his knowledge. A couple of detectives were established in an apartment near his with orders to keep a protective eye on him. Fiorello found out about it somehow and hit the roof. He summoned the detectives to his office. "Very well," he said, "at the expense of the *taxpayers* you're protecting me. Where was I last night at eight-thirty?" They didn't know. "I was hiding out," Fiorello told them acidly, "in a front box at the opera. Five thousand other people knew where I was, but not you two. I guess you must be the same detectives that looked for Dutch Schultz."

Savage is the word for Fiorello's feeling about gangsters. His instructions to the Police Department were, in effect, Be sure you've got the right man, then give him the works. This ruthless point of view exercised several civil liberties groups, and protests were lodged regarding irregular police procedure. Fiorello once called Valentine over to City Hall to face one such group. "Louie," he said, "these people claim you violate the Constitution." "So do the gangsters," said Valentine. Fiorello nodded, much pleased, and dismissed the petitioners forthwith.

There is no doubt that Fiorello did in fact go far beyond constitutional limitations in his unremitting war on gangsterism. Inside or outside the legal framework, however, he never deviated an inch. When it became common knowledge that a notorious criminal by the name of Terranova was in effect barred from New York by an order for his detainment at the city limits, a delegation of Liberals protested. Their argument was that if every mayor did the same it could become an arbitrary injustice that would put a stop to freedom of movement in the United States. "You're absolutely correct," Fiorello told the body; and, turning to his Police Commissioner, he added: "Terranova has a perfect right to come into New York City. Let him come in, by all means! *Wait until he gets to 125th Street —and then go to work on him.*"

His standards for police action were almost the same as for an armed reconnaissance patrol in time of war. One time a thug had got the drop on a Jersey City cop, and at pistol point the patrolman had yielded up his own weapon. Mayor Hague of Jersey City condoned it; he said the cop had had no alternative to surrendering his pistol. Fiorello at once issued an order to New York's Finest that this philosophy was not in their tradition—that they should yield their lives before yielding their guns. He said he expected them to shoot it out under any and all circumstances. It was what Fiorello would have done himself if he were a cop. The order made me think of his scathing attack on Dutch Schultz in 1931. The gangster numbered among his friends powerful Bronx officials and even sported a deputy sheriff's badge. The papers blazoned Fiorello's disparaging remarks, and there was muttering to the effect that the outspoken Congressman was a candidate for a bullet. I felt a little alarm, and one night, after a particularly blistering attack on New York judges who had gangster pals, I insisted on walking home with him. He wanted to know why. I didn't want to tell him, but he pressed me and I finally said I was afraid he might get shot at. He looked very tired. Then he brightened up and said, "Oh, well, a bullet in the head is a good way to die."

By and large, though, Fiorello thoroughly enjoyed himself as Mayor. His office gave him plenty of opportunity to indulge his fondness for the spotlight. Leading a contingent of New York policemen in a Washington, D.C., parade was a routine gratification, but conducting the combined Police and Sanitation departments' bands to a capacity Carnegie Hall audience was meat and drink. The city was virtually tied up for days as its two key departments braced themselves for the ordeal. Everybody was afraid that Fiorello the Conductor might let loose on them as Fiorello the Mayor. The stage manager of this stupendous spectacle took no chances and went down to City Hall for final instructions. He asked Fiorello how he wanted the spotlights used. "Shall I play them on you as you come down the aisle, and follow you right up to the podium, Mr. Mayor?"

"Hell, no!" said Fiorello. "Just treat me like Toscanini!"

Though it was a very real wrench for me, the time had come for our paths—Fiorello's and mine—to divide. I had been admitted to the Bar in January of 1932 and had hung out my shingle at a little office of my own. From that point on I had doubled in brass, spending most of my days in Fiorello's office and working at night on my own affairs, which were in no way connected with Fiorello. I was lucky from the start; friends of mine who were handling some international matters asked me to look into certain conflicts of tax law for them and my personal scene shifted increasingly to Washington. A great many Columbia men, headed for the most part by Adolf Berle, were invoked into F.D.R.'s kitchen Cabinet, and my connections with several of them were close. I practically lived in Washington during most of 1933, commuting to New York as I could. I saw very little of Fiorello after he became Mayor, but I knew most of his close advisers, and I enjoyed following the repercussions emanating from the City Hall in New York, some of which were felt in Washington itself. Fiorello's formal biographer will have no trouble researching his twelve years as New York's finest Mayor; the whole story may be found in the headlines of the city's papers, and a remarkable story it is—one in which the whole country may take pardonable pride.

But we kept in touch. Once I sent him a teasing note urging him to do New York City the favor of starting Daylight Saving as far before the June equinox as it extended after it. I pointed out that this would enable the city's populace to enjoy long spring afternoons. The whole thing was worded in very technical language which I all but copied out of a meteorological text at my elbows—the point being that of *course* Fiorello would know what the highly specialized terminology meant. It got the rise I had hoped for: back came my note with the following message scribbled in the margin: "Ernest: Wait till I finish reforming the Constitution, and *then* I'll go after the damn' solar system. F. La G."

XIV

He became a legend in his lifetime. As is the case with most legends, a hard core of truth at the center lent weight and substance to the gaudy ornament of popular illusion: Fiorello really was the kind of man he was reputed to be; the myth and the reality were one and the same in almost every particular. What people might not have appreciated, however, was the fact that the myth was painstakingly fashioned by the great man himself. For the spectacular production that was Fiorello H. La Guardia, Fiorello provided the script, the direction, and the star performer. That there was nothing bogus about his motives or techniques does not affect the shrewd, calculated showmanship that characterized the whole shebang. David Belasco was no more skillful than Fiorello in his ability to get exactly the effects he desired. Like all good artists, Fiorello never lost sight of his audience. He made his audience, indeed, an integral part of the act. Kipling called this talent the Common Touch—which, even in superior people, is really the most uncommon touch of all—the touch of genius itself.

In a good many ways, Fiorello was way ahead of his audience, but he always translated his ideas into language his audience understood. He has been accused of being a demagogue, but his election speeches indicate that he had merely developed communication in the form of its lowest common denominators—and that's how elections are won. For every ounce of entertainment Fiorello supplied, he provided a pound of instruction. Nobody ever called him an egghead, but that's what he was: an unconfused liberal convinced of the righteousness of his goals and possessed of the power to attain them. Because of his very real gifts of intellect, of character and personality, he stood against the backdrop of his times like a giant—and was artist enough to make the most of it. And because the larger than life-size part had authenticity as well as drama, people responded to it. As he thought of it, it wasn't a case of an actor playing the role of a Man of Destiny; it was Destiny playing the role of a Man.

An old Italian once said, "Fiorello is working for the biggest funeral in the history of New York." It was the sort of thing you could say about him if you didn't really believe it. Certainly he worked hard—drove himself and others—in his determination to be known as an important figure in American history and the best Mayor New York ever had. But these were not ends in themselves for him; they were only indications that he was successfully fulfilling that higher purpose that informed his whole life. And no one can say he failed, though he himself might not agree that he had succeeded.

World War II drove our paths further apart than ever. I was liaison for the O.S.S. with British Security and the

F.B.I., and such was the pressure of current events that I had no time for the past. Neither, of course, had Fiorello. Shortly after the end of the war, Colonel David "Mickey" Marcus dropped in on me one evening in Washington. Mickey had been Fiorello's Commissioner of Correction (prisons) and we talked for hours about our old boss. Mickey had had it rough; the city's prisons were a mess when Fiorello took over—run in many cases as though they were private concessions for the guards, who, for a price, would cater to every demand from dope to homosexuality. It had been Mickey's job to clean up this sewer and put the prisons on the same basis as the hospital system, with emphasis on efficiency, no favoritism and no cruelty. Such was Fiorello's demonic fervor that it was almost a relief for Mickey to escape into the uniform of an Army colonel when the war came along. But of course he couldn't really get away from Fiorello any more than the rest of us. Mark Clark had just taken over Naples, and Mickey was made a military governor. In this capacity he received a cablegram from Fiorello reading: "Reliably informed 150,000 women and children without shoes Naples area. Demand explanation."

Mickey cabled back: "We took over this city only 24 hours ago and we sure as hell didn't steal them"—and received the reply:

"I want a good explanation, not a poor excuse."

The last time I was to see Fiorello was in Paris in the summer of 1946, during the Paris Conference. He was in Europe as head of UNRRA. Captain Joe Lilly, his aide, had told me that he was the same old dynamo, raising hell all day long. "I'm having a terrible time," Joe said. "He runs me ragged." I could believe it. With the task of feeding, clothing, and housing millions of starving, wretched people, and with the means of doing it at his disposal, I could well imagine the stringent nature of Fiorello's demands on his staff.

Joe told me one amusing story about their recent trip to Moscow together. It was arranged for Fiorello to see Stalin, and Joe asked if he could accompany him to the interview. Fiorello gave him a crushing No. Joe walked across Red Square with him, and Fiorello told him to go and look at Lenin lying in state. Joe did. By and by, Fiorello emerged from the Kremlin. As they recrossed Red Square, Joe noticed that Fiorello had a very grim air about him—head down and jaw outthrust. Finally Joe asked how he had made out. "I got from Stalin," snorted Fiorello, "what you got from Lenin! *Nothing!*"

When I walked into his characteristically plain office, however, I didn't like the way Fiorello looked. I had often seen him tired, but this was different; some of the old resilience seemed to have gone. On the surface, though, nothing had changed. He had heard that I had come to Paris from a Mediterranean area as a passenger on an Army plane, and before I even had a chance to say hello he wanted to know where I thought I got off, grabbing an Army plane for myself, and who did I think I was, anyway? The years rolled away as I explained, with a mixture of guilt and defiance, that I had merely hooked a ride in a bucket seat on a routine flight and that, furthermore, I had paid for it. He snorted but let it go.

We talked about his work with UNRRA and switched

to the political scene back home. I told him I'd heard that the New York Liberal Party planned to nominate him for Senator and that they were trying to persuade the Democrats to do the same. Fiorello shook his head and said that Boss Flynn would never permit such a thing. And he added in a most reasonable tone, "Can you blame him?" I couldn't; for years Fiorello had been an unconscionable thorn in Flynn's side.

When I stood up to go, he came around his desk and accompanied me to the door, his hand on my elbow. At the door he paused and said, "Do you know where you are?"

"What?" I asked.

"Do you know where you are?" he repeated.

"Well, sure," I said, completely at sea.

"I'll tell you where you are. You are in Paris. In *Paris*," he said sternly, gripping my arm a little tighter.

"So?"

"So," he growled, "you behave yourself, Ernest. Or I'll tell your father!"

Adolf Berle took me aside at a dinner party at his home early in September of 1947 and told me that Fiorello was dying. He had been ill for a long time and had stubbornly contested every inch of lost ground. But there was no longer any doubt as to the outcome of this, his last battle. It was only a question of time.

In the days that followed, my thoughts were full of him. And to comfort myself I took refuge in a device I had learned more than twenty years before. I call it "calipering time." An old gentleman whose cigar I had lighted during an intermission at the Palace Theater taught it to me.

When he heard I was majoring in history at Columbia, he said, "Let me give you some history to think about." And, briefly, he told me some fascinating details about the siege of Rochelle, three hundred years ago. "That story," he concluded, "was told to me when I was a little boy by my grandfather. He had heard the story as a little boy from *his* grandfather, who actually witnessed the siege. So there you are—an eyewitness account from only three men to you of something that happened three centuries ago."

Somehow I felt I had been handed a key to something vastly important. Three hundred years—three men. There were only seven such periods between me and Caesar! By "calipering" those three hundred years ahead, that would be the year 2226. I had the strange sensation of occupying the exact center of a six-hundred-year span. It was like the discovery of a new dimension; it gave me a feeling of solidity, of permanence and continuity, of purpose. This "calipering" may be of no validity to anyone except me, but for me it has been, as I say, a most comforting concept.

Fiorello had been born in 1882, sixty-five years before. Calipered ahead from the present, his life span reached the year 2012; and calipered backward from the time of his birth, 1817. Nearly two centuries. And Fiorello in the midst of it. It is improbable that he will be called the Man of the Century, but assuredly he was a Twentieth Century Man, as uniquely so as Michelangelo was a Renaissance Man.

I doubt that Fiorello himself would have put much stock in my time calipers. His was a rigidly practical turn of mind, not easily given to free flights of fancy. Once, when we were having a quiet drink together, I muttered the first line of a poem I had always liked. "Poetry." He sniffed. "Well, go on with it." I did:

> " 'They told me, Heraclitus, they told me you
> were dead,
> They brought me bitter news to hear and bitter
> tears to shed.
> I wept as I remember'd how often you and I
> Had tired the sun with talking and sent him
> down the sky.
>
> " 'And now that thou art lying, my dear old Ca-
> rian guest,
> A handful of gray ashes, long, long ago at rest,
> Still are thy pleasant voices, thy nightingales,
> awake;
> For Death, he taketh all away, but them he can-
> not take.' "

When I finished, Fiorello said simply, "He didn't want to see his friend die."

"No," I said. "He didn't."

"Well," said Fiorello, "you can't blame him for that."

"No," I said. "You can't."

Berle called me on September 20th and told me Fiorello was dead. In the split second after I heard the news, I was transported in time and space to a certain golden autumn afternoon before the war on the crest of a hill near Pound Ridge in Westchester. I was riding a huge, splendid Canadian hunter named Wotan, who had a heart like a lion and could soar over fences like an arrow in flight. It was very warm. We had taken a wrong trail and were separated from the rest of the party. Alone, we clattered up a stony path and, after a brief run, burst out of the trees onto the northern slope of a steep hill. At the summit I pulled up the heaving beast and we stood still, both of us drinking in the cool fresh breeze.

My eyes are very sensitive to light. Autumn sunshine has a peculiarly distinctive quality for me. Everything seems limned in clearest tones, as though each tree and bush were a sharply delineated silhouette in a Japanese water color. The turning foliage of fall always makes me think of a magnificent but doomed army. The first dry leaves that spiral to the ground seem to me like the first casualties of a disastrous engagement. A forest in autumn is a great, embattled host, fearless in the face of certain death, like Braddock in his Red Coat, mounting a gun caisson to direct the fire in a hopeless cause and accepting, as a Coldstreamer should, the idea of death with the same sangfroid he would feel for any dress parade.

From the top of the hill I absorbed the whole pageantry of fall. Wotan was motionless, like a statue cast in bronze. Ahead of us stretched a green field, and in the middle of it stood a single gigantic maple like a proud torch of scarlet and yellow. Its leaves quivered in the crystal-clear autumn light like the battle flags of an assembly of Scottish clans. The tree was a haughty warrior, contemptuous of the timid grass that seemed to be fleeing in panic before the foe as the wind swept across the field. The warrior might die, but he would not be conquered. It would stand like a man until the last wintry blast would topple it and wrench out its roots.

Berle was saying: "What was that, Ernie? I didn't catch it."

"Nothing," I said into the phone. "I was just thinking about a tree. A tree that reminded me of Fiorello."